DEEP INNER PEACE

Jack Hartman

Library of Congress Catalog Card Number 84-073323

"Thy Word is a *lamp*
unto my
feet, and a *light*
unto my pathway."

Psalm 119:105

First Printing - 12/84 - 20,000 copies

Published by:

LAMPLIGHT PUBLICATIONS

P.O. Box 3293   Manchester, New Hampshire 03105

Designed and Produced by Custom Graphics, Tulsa, Oklahoma

Contents

Introduction

At the age of 43 I found myself facing two very real problems — financial bankruptcy and an emotional breakdown. In our book *Trust God For Your Finances* I explained in detail what God's Word teaches about solving financial problems. In this book, I'd like to share what I have learned from God's Word about overcoming emotional problems by finding God's deep inner peace—a peace that is *so great* that it cannot be grasped within the limits of the human mind.

Let's start by examining the three words "deep inner peace." First of all, I have looked up the Greek and Hebrew words that are translated "peace" in the Bible. In broad terms, the translation of these words can be summarized as "harmony between God and man, harmony between one another and harmony deep down inside of ourselves."

Webster's New World Dictionary defines the word "deep" as "...extending inward from the surface...strongly felt...greater degree of intensity...". Webster defines "inner" as "...located farther within...of the mind or the spirit...more intimate." Webster defines the word "peace" as "...freedom from disagreements or quarrels...harmony...an undisturbed state of mind...absence of mental conflict...serenity...calm, quiet tranquility...".

I have combined these definitions for the following definition of "deep inner peace" that we'll be studying in this book. I would define "deep inner peace" as *"the strong, intense inner spiritual calmness that we receive from being in harmony with our Creator, with one another and with ourselves."*

Everyone has a strong desire for deep inner peace. With all of the disturbing problems in the world today, there has never been a greater need for this peace. Our lives seem to get more complicated with each passing year. We live in a fast-moving, anxious world. Most of us have to deal with more pressure today than we did ten years ago and expect to face even more pressure in the future.

Many, many Christians who will live eternally at peace in heaven are missing out on the peace that Jesus Christ left for us here on this earth— "Peace I leave with you, *my peace I give unto you: not* as the world giveth, give I unto you. Let *not* your heart be troubled, *neither* let it be afraid" (John 14:27). Jesus gave us His peace to use *now*— right here in the middle of this restless, troubled, pressure-packed world.

Christians will automatically live in God's peace when we get to heaven, but this peace *isn't* "automatic" here on earth. God's Word tells us to search eagerly for this peace—"...*search* for peace— harmony, undisturbedness from fears, agitating passions and moral conflicts—and seek it *eagerly*. Do not merely desire peaceful relations [with God, with your fellowmen, and with yourself], but *pursue*, go after them!" (I Peter 3:11, *The Amplified Bible).*

An abundance of peace is available to us now.

God's Word says that He "...will reveal unto them the *abundance of peace* and truth" (Jeremiah 33:6). It tells us exactly what we need to do if we want to experience His deep inner peace in our lives. We need to follow His instructions—"Let us therefore *follow after the things* which make for peace..." (Romans 14:19).

We all want deep inner peace, but very few of us know how to obtain it. We can only experience it if we learn God's laws pertaining to peace and then follow them in our everyday lives.

I ask each person reading this book to ask yourself three questions:

1) *Do I* sincerely want to experience deep inner peace in my life?

2) If so, *what* specific laws of God do I *now know* that will show me how to obtain it?

3) *Am I willing* to pay a very *definite* price over a *long* period of time to learn and apply my Father's instructions for deep inner peace?

Virtually everyone will answer the first question "yes." However, if we're really honest about the second question, most of us will have to admit that we don't know more than a few isolated verses of Scripture about the subject of peace.

That brings us to the third question—what price are we really willing to pay in order to experience God's deep inner peace in our lives??? God's great truths about peace are so overwhelming that they can't be understood with our minds. These truths must be spiritually discerned. Too many of us simply aren't paying the price to open ourselves up to the great truths that are available to us. We see and we hear, but we don't understand. The following words could apply to many of us:

"...You will indeed hear and hear with your ears, but will *not* understand; and you will indeed look and look with your eyes, but will not see—*not* perceive, have knowledge of or become acquainted with what you look at, at all. For the *heart*—the understanding, the soul—of this people has grown dull (stupid, hardened and calloused) and their ears are heavy and hard of hearing, and they have shut tight their eyes, so that they may *not* perceive and have knowledge and become acquainted with their eyes, and hear with their ears, and understand with their souls..." (Acts 28:26-27, *The Amplified Bible).*

In this book we'll study our Father's detailed instructions which will show us how to manifest the great peace that our Lord Jesus has given to us. Will you open up your eyes and ears? Are you really willing to pay the price of continual study and meditation in God's Word? This book will be like an "encyclopedia" on the subject of peace. We'll study hundreds of verses of Scripture that will show us *exactly* how to find the deep inner peace that is available to us.

God's Word teaches that peace is a fruit of His Holy Spirit. "...the fruit of the Spirit is love, joy, *peace...*" (Galatians 5:22). In order to enjoy fruit, we have to plant seeds. Then the seeds have to grow. This is true in the agricultural realm and it is equally true in the spiritual realm. If we want to enjoy the fruit of peace in our lives, we must plant the seeds of peace. Then we have to cultivate this fruit over a period of time so that it will grow properly.

In the spiritual realm, God's Word is a *seed*— "...The seed is the word of God" (Luke 8:11). We need to plant this seed in our hearts through constant, patient study and meditation. This is how we produce fruit—"...these are [the people] who hearing the Word, hold it fast in a just—noble, virtuous—and worthy heart, and *steadily bring*

10

forth fruit with patience" (Luke 8:15, *The Amplified Bible).*

This is the only way to receive the fruit of deep inner peace. The seeds will take root and grow to the exact degree that we study and meditate and then *do* what God's Word says, "...receive and welcome the Word which *implanted* and *rooted [in your hearts]* contains the power to save your souls. But—*obey* the message; be *doers* of the Word, and *not* merely listeners to it, betraying yourselves..." (James 1:21-22, *The Amplified Bible).*

God's Word tells us exactly what He wants us to do if we want to experience His deep inner peace every day of our lives. If we want to receive the peace that our Father has for us, we need to *learn* what His Word says and then *lay up* these words in our hearts—*"Acquaint now thyself* with Him, and *be at peace:* thereby good shall come unto thee. Receive, I pray thee, the law from his mouth, and *lay up his words in thine heart"* (Job 22:21-22).

God's way is the only way. Man's way is the wrong way. Our way might seem to be the right way for several years, but sooner or later we'll find that human efforts to find deep inner peace will always come up short. Sooner or later the ways that seem right to us will lead to failure—to spiritual death. "There is a way which *seemeth right* unto a man, but the end thereof are the ways of death" (Proverbs 14:12).

When we follow our human inclinations, we are always heading towards spiritual death. Spiritual life can be found only by following God's spiritual laws. We simply can't see things the way our Father sees them. His ways are much higher than our ways. "For my thoughts are *not* your thoughts, *neither* are your ways my ways, saith the Lord. For as the heavens are higher than the earth, so are my ways *higher* than your ways, and my thoughts than your thoughts" (Isaiah 55:8-9).

In this book we'll study His higher ways in detail and we'll carefully outline His specific instructions for deep inner peace.

Chapter One

The World's Way Or God's Way?

All over the world, people are searching for peace. In our attempt to deal with the many frustrations caused by family problems, health problems, financial problems and other problems of our generation, all of us look for relief.

Some people go to extremes—illegal drugs, alcohol and sexual relationships outside of marriage. They grasp at any straw for a few hours of relaxation. Others follow more traditional means and try to find a peaceful existence through tranquilizers and other prescribed drugs. All of us seek relief through hobbies and vacations.

Never in the history of mankind has a generation of people tried so hard to find peace through external activities. We go to the beach, to the mountains and to sporting events. We watch television, we go to the movies and to restaurants and clubs. We try to find what we're looking for in new cars, new homes and new boats. There have never been more people fishing, hunting, camping, golfing and playing tennis. Travel agencies tell us about trips by plane, train, boat or car to Florida, California, Bermuda, Hawaii, Europe and other beautiful places.

Is all of this wrong? Am I saying that Christians shouldn't do these things?? Of course not!! There isn't anything wrong with engaging in hobbies and wholesome worldly pleasures as long as they don't get out of balance. However, *nothing* should come ahead of God.

Families, hobbies and other interests are all fine—*if* they take a distant second place to the Lord Jesus Christ, who should be the absolute center of our lives all day long, every day of our lives. Unfortunately, though, millions of people (including many Christians) are much more caught up with worldly activities than they are with the Lord.

Various sources of recreation should *supplement* our spiritual source of peace, but they should *not* be our primary source for trying to obtain peace. We cannot find lasting peace externally. Too many of us are looking outside of ourselves for peace that can only be found deep down inside. We'll never experience this peace unless we give the Lord His rightful place in our lives—*first place*...ahead of family, friends, hobbies and everything else.

We'll never find peace in activities, people, places or things, but this is where the world continually looks for peace. The world's system for finding peace can be successful in wiping problems out of our minds for a few hours. *Don't* call this peace, though. It is *postponement!*

Amusement has become a multi-trillion dollar business. Movie stars, television celebrities and professional athletes are receiving salaries that would have been incomprehensible just a few short years ago. Why are they making so much money? They're receiving these tremendous incomes because of insatiable demands for amusement and recreation from a world that is frantically looking for escape from the problems of life. We spend more money on entertainment than any generation in history, yet there have never been anywhere near as many troubled people as there are now.

God didn't create us so that we would be able to find true peace in the world of our senses. God's Word tells us that we won't receive any lasting satisfaction from this realm. "...the eye is *not* satisfied with seeing, *nor* the ear filled with hearing" (Ecclesiastes 1:8). In the world of the senses, the more we get, the more we want. "...the lust of the eyes of man is *never* satisfied" (Proverbs 27:20, *The Amplified Bible*). When we constantly lust after more than we have, these lustful desires stop us from enjoying what God has already given us.

The external relief that we chase after is temporary. God is eternal. We won't find peace unless we turn away from the temporary pleasures of the world and turn instead to the lasting eternal peace and quietness of God who never changes. "For I am the Lord, I *change not...*" (Malachi 3:6).

God's Word tells us that we shouldn't do things the way that the world does."Do *not* be conformed to this world—this age, fashioned after and adapted to its *external, superficial customs...*" (Romans 12:2, *The Amplified Bible*). Worldly people don't know how to find deep inner peace. Neither will we if we follow their ways. The following words that Isaiah spoke to the Israelites could apply to us today: "*You don't know* what *true peace* is, nor what it means to be just and good; you continually do *wrong* and those who follow you *won't* experience *any peace*, either" (Isaiah 59:8, *The Living Bible*).

Our Father's peace is in a class by itself just as our Father is in a class by Himself. The world's ways can't even begin to compare to His ways of finding peace. Lasting peace doesn't come from the accumulation of property. In fact, this accumulation blocks us from obtaining peace. Lasting peace doesn't come from fame and fortune. It's obvious that many people have everything that money can buy, but they aren't at peace. There is no way that discontented people can find contentment from riches and fame.

Truly rich people are those people who have found peace *within themselves.* The world's peace comes *in* from the *outside.* God's peace comes *out* from the *inside.* We must find internal peace before we can enjoy external peace.

Our Father's peace can't be purchased. All of His blessings are priceless and can only be obtained by surrendering ourselves to Him and following His directions. "Wait and listen, every one who is thirsty! Come to the waters; and he who has no money, come, buy and eat! Yes, come, buy priceless [spiritual] wine and milk *without money* and *without price* [simply for the self-surrender that accepts the blessing]. *Why* do you spend your money for that which is not bread? And your earnings for what *does not satisfy?* Hearken diligently *to Me,* and eat what is good, and let your soul *delight itself* in fatness [the profuseness of spiritual joy]. Incline your ear [submit and consent to the Divine will], and *come to Me;* hear, and your soul shall *revive..."* (Isaiah 55:1-3, *The Amplified Bible).*

Why do Christians chase after worldly substitutes when "the real thing" is available to us??? The world's peace is dependent upon eliminating problems. The peace of God, however, doesn't change in the least, no matter how severe our problems might be. Henry Drummond, Dr. Billy Graham and other Christian teachers have compared the world's version of peace with God's peace by telling a story of two artists who were asked to paint a picture of peace.

One artist painted a picture of a beautiful, still, sunny lake surrounded by mountains. The lake was calm and tranquil and its blue waters reflected the beautiful sun. This is the world's version of peace. The other artist painted a picture of a violent, raging storm. In the midst of the storm on a branch of a tree was a bird's nest. In that nest was a small bird sleeping—totally oblivious to the turmoil around it. This is God's peace. The cover of this book shows our artist's conception of this deep inner peace.

Peace that is based upon external conditions is extremely fragile. Some of us lose our fragile peace simply by listening to a weather forecast that spoils our plans for a relaxed outing. How can we enjoy deep inner peace if little things like weather reports upset us? Some of us are disturbed when we learn that someone has said an uncomplimentary thing about us. How can we enjoy deep inner peace if we're shaken up because someone says something that we don't like?

The world's peace is tied to the balance in our bank accounts, how we feel, how our wives (or husbands) are treating us and how our children are doing. The world's peace can be vastly different between Friday night and Monday morning than it is during the rest of the week.

Any peace that is governed by external conditions is at the mercy of change and chance. This kind of peace isn't realistic. There is only one place where everything always goes well and that is heaven. Life in this world is full of problems. Peace that is based upon the absence of problems is a fleeting, brittle peace that lacks a solid foundation.

The world's peace will never stand the test of time. It is hollow. The aging process will always demonstrate this. As we grow older, sooner or later a severe lack of peace will disrupt the lives of all who trust in and love this world. It may take awhile, but it will happen.

The world's peace looks great when we're in green pastures and beside still waters, but we must have the peace of God to sustain us when we go through the dark valleys. Deep inner peace comes only from our Creator. God's Word tells us how to find this peace. "...to be *spiritually minded* is life and *peace*" (Romans 8:6). There is only one way to find deep inner peace and that is in the spiritual realm. This peace is only available to the spiritually-minded.

As we search for what God's Word says about deep inner peace, let's start by studying peace *with* God. There is no way that we can enjoy *the peace of God* unless we first of all have *peace with God.*

Chapter 2

Peace With God

Many of us don't realize that inner peace and peace with other people, first of all, must be preceded by peace with God. We can't have the peace of God until, first of all, we are at peace with God. This is the foundation of all peace.

There are two kinds of people in the world— people who have accepted Jesus Christ as their Saviour and people who haven't. God's Word says that people who have not repented from their sins and accepted Jesus as their Saviour *cannot* receive the peace of God. These people might look good on the outside, but deep down inside, they're *not* at peace. They're like the sea in a storm—churning and troubled, constantly digging up dirt from deep down inside of themselves. "...the wicked are like the troubled sea, for it *cannot* rest and its waters cast up mire and dirt. There is *no peace,* says my God, for the wicked" (Isaiah 57:20-21, *The Amplified Bible).*

What does the word "wicked" mean? The Hebrew word that is translated "wicked" in Isaiah 57:21 actually means "unrighteous." Since the word "righteous" refers to those who are in right standing with God, the word "unrighteous" means those who are not in right standing with God. So, this

19

verse of Scripture really tells us that God's peace is not available to those who are not in right standing with Him.

Some people who have not accepted Jesus as their Saviour seem to live good lives. However, no matter how good their lives might seem to be, God's Word tells us that, with the exception of Jesus Christ, every person who has ever lived is a sinner. "For *all* have sinned, and come short of the glory of God..." (Romans 3:23). None of us are righteous unless Jesus Christ is our Saviour. "...There is *none* righteous, no, *not one*" (Romans 3:10).

Why is this? It all started with Adam. He lived a beautiful life in the Garden of Eden and he fellowshipped often with God and enjoyed His peace. However, Adam rebelled against God and, as a result, he became separated from God. Peace means "one with God" and when Adam's disobedience separated him from God, he lost the peace that he had. For the first time in his life, he experienced fear. "...I was afraid..." (Genesis 3:10).

How does this affect us? All of us are affected because "...Adam's sin brought punishment to *all*..." (Romans 5:18, *The Living Bible).* With the exception of Jesus Christ, every person who has lived on this earth since Adam's fall is a descendant of Adam. We all inherited Adam's sin and, as a result, all of us were born as sinners separated from God. "...We started out bad, being *born with evil natures...*" (Ephesians 2:3, *The Living Bible).* No matter how good we might think we are, *all* of us are sinners in God's eyes. Anyone who disagrees with this disagrees with the Word of God!

God sent His only Son, Jesus Christ, to earth to enable us to receive freedom from Adam's sin. Jesus came to this earth to die for our sins and He rose from the dead to put every one who accepts

Him as Saviour back into right standing with God (righteousness). "He died for our sins and rose again to make us *right with God...*" (Romans 4:25, *The Living Bible*). Because of this, Jesus gave all of us the opportunity to become perfect in God's sight. "...by that one offering He made *forever perfect* in the sight of God all those whom He is making holy" (Hebrews 10:14, *The Living Bible*).

We cannot fully comprehend what it means to be at peace with God unless we first understand the magnitude of God's love for us. God loves everyone in this world so much that He gave His only Son so that none of us would have to go to hell. "For God *so loved* the world, that he gave his only begotten Son, that whosoever believeth in him should *not* perish, but have *everlasting* life" (John 3:16).

The magnitude of God's love is beyond human comprehension. How many earthly parents would give their only son to die a horrible death the way that our Father gave up his only Son?? God performed this great act of love for everyone in the world—not only for Christians, but also for atheists who hate Him and deny Him, for murderers, rapists, thieves and all other sinners. "...God *shows* and clearly *proves* His [own] love for us by the fact that *while we were still sinners* Christ, the Messiah, the Anointed One, died for us" (Romans 5:8, *The Amplified Bible*).

God loves us more than we can comprehend. Jesus loves us more than we can comprehend. *How much* does Jesus love us? Just try and visualize Jesus—God Himself—hanging on the cross—dirty, sweaty and naked—with a crown of thorns on His head, spikes driven through His hands and feet, and blood dripping from His mutilated back. Visualize this picture and listen to Jesus saying directly to you, *"I love you this much!"*

Jesus paid our price for us. He gave Himself as our ransom. "...Christ Jesus; who gave himself a *ransom* for all..." (I Timothy 2:5-6). This is the greatest act of love that the world has ever known—"God showed how much He loved us by sending His only Son into this wicked world to bring to us eternal life through His death. In this act we see what *real love* is..." (I John 4:9-10, *The Living Bible*).

Jesus was wounded because of our sins and His suffering made it possible for us to be at peace with God. "...he was wounded and bruised for our sins. He was chastised *that we might have peace...*" (Isaiah 53:5, *The Living Bible*). Jesus is our peace. "...He is [Himself] *our peace*—our bond of unity and harmony..." (Ephesians 2:14, *The Amplified Bible*).

Because of what Jesus did, it is possible for every one of us to be at peace with Almighty God. It is possible to be acquitted from all of our sins and brought into right standing with God and to enjoy the beautiful peace that this reconciliation makes possible. "...since we are justified—acquitted, declared righteous, and given a right standing with God—through faith, let us [grasp the fact that we] have *[the peace of reconciliation]* to hold and to enjoy, *peace with God* through our Lord Jesus Christ, the Messiah, the Anointed One" (Romans 5:1, *The Amplified Bible*).

Jesus *restored* the peace that Adam lost. He is in charge of all peace. Because of this, He is called "The Prince of Peace." There is no end—no limit—to the peace that is available through Him. "For unto us a child is born, unto us a son is given: and the government shall be upon his shoulder: and his name shall be called Wonderful, Counsellor, The mighty God, The everlasting Father, *The Prince of Peace.* Of the increase of his government and peace *there shall be no end..."* (Isaiah 9:6-7).

We don't receive God's peace by going to church regularly and living a good life. There is only one way to receive the deep inner peace, serenity, quietness and harmony that comes from oneness with God and that is through Jesus Christ. "Jesus said to him, I am the Way and the Truth and the Life; *no one* comes to the Father except by (through) Me" (John 14:6, *The Amplified Bible*).

When we accept Jesus as our Saviour, we are able to find the peace that the whole world is searching for. "Therefore if any man be in Christ, he is a new creature: old things are passed away; *behold, all things are become new*" (II Corinthians 5:17). Our lives can be transformed beyond our comprehension by accepting Jesus as our Saviour. We can enter into eternal peace with our Father— peace that is not available in any other way.

Perhaps some readers of this book might wonder what I mean by accepting Jesus as our Saviour. If so, please turn to the Appendix at the end of this book which is titled "Have You Entered Into The Kingdom Of God?" This Appendix explains exactly how we enter into the kingdom of God by receiving eternal salvation as a result of accepting Jesus Christ as our Saviour.

No matter how evil we might have been, our penalty has been paid. We can come into our Father's presence with perfect peace. "...Christ's death on the cross has made *peace with God* for *all* by His blood. This *includes* you who were once so far away from God. You were His enemies and hated Him and were separated from Him by your evil thoughts and actions, yet now He has brought you back as His friends. He has done this through the death on the cross of His own human body, and now as a result Christ has brought you into the very presence of God, and you are standing there before Him with *nothing* left against you—nothing left that He could even chide you for; the only condition is that you fully believe the Truth, standing in it steadfast and firm, strong in the Lord, convinced of the Good News that Jesus died for you, and never shifting from trusting Him to save you. This is the wonderful news that came to each of you and is now spreading all over the world..." (Colossians 1:20-23, *The Living Bible).*

Jesus paid the price that enables us to be brought into right standing with God. As long as we know deep down inside of ourselves that we are in right standing with our Father, we will be filled with quiet, confident peace. "...the effect of righteousness shall be *peace* [internal and external], and the result of righteousness, *quietness* and *confident trust for ever"* (Isaiah 32:17, *The Amplified Bible).*

When we accept Jesus as our Saviour, this brings us into a position of peace with God. After that great decision, if we sin, we can go to our Father and confess our sins. When we do this with a repentant heart, He will forgive us and cleanse us from our sins, thus maintaining our beautiful peace with Him. "If we confess our sins, he is faithful and just to *forgive* us our sins, and to *cleanse* us from *all* unrighteousness" (I John 1:9).

In this chapter, we have seen how we can obtain peace with God. *All* Christians have this peace *with* God. Unfortunately, many Christians *aren't* enjoying the peace *of* God. Many Christians are living with the same tension, anxiety and stress that non-believers live with. We don't have to put up with all of these emotional disturbances if we'll learn and follow the instructions that our Father's Book of Instructions gives to us.

Chapter 3

The Peace Of God

Peace *with God* and *the peace of God* are quite different. We receive the peace of God each day of our lives only to the degree that we follow the instructions that our Father has given us in His Word.

Jesus Christ has given the peace of God to every Christian. Jesus is God and He clearly told us, "Peace I leave with you; *My [own] peace* I now give and bequeath to you. *Not* as the world gives do I give to you. *Do not let* your heart be troubled, neither let it be *afraid—stop* allowing yourselves to be agitated and disturbed; and do *not* permit yourselves to be fearful and intimidated and cowardly and unsettled" (John 14:27, *The Amplified Bible).*

These are powerful words! Do you know when Jesus said them? He said them in the "upper room" at the last supper. Jesus knew where He was going when He left that room. He knew that He soon would sweat blood at Gethsemane before being brutally whipped by Roman soldiers. He knew that He would suffer terrible, excruciating pain and then death by crucifixion. With full knowledge of the ordeal He was about to face, Jesus not only maintained His peace, but He also passed it on to His disciples urging them not to be afraid just as He was not afraid.

I ask each person reading this book, *do you* allow yourself to be troubled, afraid, agitated or disturbed?? It's interesting to see what Jesus said about that. He told us that we shouldn't *let* ourselves be troubled or afraid. He told us that we shouldn't *allow* ourselves to be agitated and disturbed. He told us that we shouldn't *permit* ourselves to be fearful, intimidated, cowardly and unsettled.

These three words, "let," "allow" and "permit" have one thing in common. They show us that *we* have the option to *choose!* We choose whether or not we are going to let fear come into our lives. We choose whether or not we are going to allow ourselves to be intimidated.

It's up to us to decide if we will allow fear and worry to rule us or whether we allow the peace of God to rule us. "...*let* the peace (soul harmony which comes) from the Christ *rule* (act as umpire continually) in your hearts—deciding and settling with finality all questions that arise in your minds..." (Colossians 3:15, *The Amplified Bible*).

We don't have to choose worry and fear. Instead, God's Word tells us that we should choose His peace—the beautiful harmony that exists in our souls when Jesus Christ truly is in charge of our lives. If we *truly do* surrender every aspect of our lives each day to Jesus Christ, then *why* would we *ever* be afraid??

He lives in our hearts and we should turn to Him allowing Him to settle any and all problems that arise in our lives. The original Greek in Colossians 3:15 says that His peace is to be the "umpire." An umpire rules an athletic contest—he is in control of it. Our Father says that, *instead* of being worried or afraid, we should allow His peace to *control* our lives.

When we're confronted with a crisis, we shouldn't allow ourselves to panic. Our hearts and minds should be so full of God's Word that we automatically will react to it instead of reacting to the circumstances that we are faced with or to our emotions. This is why the next verse tells us, *"Let the word* [spoken by] the Christ, the Messiah, *have its home* (in your hearts and minds) and *dwell in you* in [all its] richness..."* (Colossians 3:16, *The Amplified Bible).*

We have been given a very unique peace—the peace of Jesus Christ. As we read the four gospels that tell us about His life, we can clearly see that His peace is absolutely majestic. In spite of all the insults, accusations and beatings that He had to face, Jesus never lost His peace and composure. No matter what happened to Him He remained calm. He—"Never answered back when insulted; when He suffered He did not threaten to get even; He left His case in the hands of God who always judges fairly" (I Peter 2:23, *The Living Bible).*

This is the peace that Jesus gave us! He gave us the *same* peace that He took to the cross—the peace that never once lost its composure as He hung on the cross, aching with pain, listening to the many insults that were flung at Him by a jeering crowd of onlookers. In spite of this, Jesus maintained His peace and said, "...Father, forgive them; for they know not what they do..." (Luke 23:34).

This *same* peace has been given to us to sustain us during trials and tribulations. Jesus doesn't want us worrying and struggling. He wants us to trust in the peace that He has given us. We need to take our minds off the problems in our lives and fix them instead on the magnificent peace and calmness of Jesus Christ who lives in our hearts.

Human peace is surface peace. Sooner or later,

we'll come across challenges and setbacks that will overwhelm any peace that we can manufacture for ourselves. This is why Jesus gave us His peace. He did this for the same reason that you and I give gifts to people—He gave us His peace because He wants us to *use* it. Unfortunately, millions of Christians don't use this gift that Jesus has given to us. This fact is very obvious simply by observing the actions of many Christians.

We should test ourselves against John 14:27. Do we let our hearts be troubled or afraid? Do we allow ourselves to be agitated and disturbed? Do we permit ourselves to be intimidated, cowardly and unsettled? Most of us probably have to answer at least a qualified "yes" to these questions. The truth is that a great majority of Christians don't even come close to living in the peace that has been given to us.

Jesus has given us all the peace that we'll ever need. Why is it that so many Christians aren't receiving this peace? We fail to experience it because we, a) *don't know* what God's Word says about peace and/or, b) *don't believe deeply* and act in total faith on what God's Word says about it.

Our Lord Jesus was sent to this earth "...to *guide* our feet into the way of *peace*" (Luke 1:79). He has done His part. He has given us His strength. He has blessed us with peace. "The Lord will give strength unto his people; *the Lord will bless his people with peace*" (Psalm 29:11).

Our Lord's peace is available to comfort us every step of the way. It is there—just waiting for us to draw on it like money in a bank account. It is our responsibility to make "withdrawals." We receive this peace *by faith*.

The peace of God belongs to us. *We must believe that it is there simply because our Father says that it is there.* When everything is going wrong in our lives, we should calmly rely on the peace of Jesus Christ. We must dare to believe in it and receive it by faith. We need to accept by faith the peace that has been given to us. If we fill our minds and hearts with our Lord's promises on peace and meditate on them constantly, His peace will prevail in our lives.

If we aren't manifesting the peace of God in our lives we can only blame ourselves. It was given to us. It's right there waiting for us to use it. We must not block ourselves from receiving this gift because of ignorance or unbelief.

*"What does our Father do when
He finds a calm, trusting heart
that is perfect towards Him?...He
releases great power to help us."*

Chapter 4

Quiet Confidence
In The Lord

We have discussed peace with God and the peace of God. Now we're ready to discuss how to use the supernatural peace that our Lord Jesus has given us. One time that we need this peace is in times of emergency—whenever we're confronted with a crisis situation.

What do most of us do when we're suddenly faced with an emergency? We "speed up." Our heartbeat increases, our thoughts start to race and our words and actions are hurried. This is the world's way. God's way, as always, is just the opposite.

Once we have done all that we can do, our Father wants us to relax and stand solidly on our faith in Him. "...having *done all* [the crisis demands], to *stand* [firmly in your place]" (Ephesians 6:13, *The Amplified Bible*). Our Father always wants us to do our best, but then, instead of getting worried and frustrated, His Word tells us to *"Be still,* and *know* that I am God..."* (Psalm 46:10).

Whenever I'm confronted with a crisis, these eight precious words invariably come to my mind. This happens because I have spent many, many hours meditating on these wonderful words. What is our Father telling us here? First, He tells us to *be still...*to be calm, to be quiet. He tells us to calm

31

down and quiet down, to stop straining, struggling, worrying and hurrying.

Why does He tell us to "be still?" He tells us that we should be still because we *know* that He is Almighty God—the Creator of the entire universe. He is in charge. He *can* and *will* take care of everything *if* we will just let go and let Him take care of it. *Nothing* is too great for Him.

Once we have done our very best, it is foolish to panic and run around worrying and struggling. This shows lack of faith. It is a clear indication that we think that we have to do everything and we aren't trusting in the Lord.

Our Father wants us to stay calm and quiet deep down inside of ourselves. "Be *beautiful inside*, in your hearts, with the lasting charm of a *gentle and quiet spirit* which is so precious to God" (I Peter 3:4, *The Living Bible*). Our Father searches for people who remain calm and confident in the midst of a crisis. "...the eyes of the Lord search back and forth across the whole earth, looking for people whose *hearts are perfect* toward him, *so that he can show his great power* in helping them..." (II Chronicles 16:9, *The Living Bible*).

When our Father's eyes go back and forth across the whole earth looking for people whose hearts are perfect toward Him, what is He looking for? He is looking for His children who remain calm, quiet and confident in spite of any crisis. He is looking for His children who never get upset because they *know* that He is God and that He is in total control at all times.

What does our Father do when He finds a calm, trusting heart that is perfect towards Him? His Word says that He releases His great power to help us. The Creator who made us in the first place is easily able to handle anything and everything that will ever come against us. "For with God *nothing is ever impossible...*" (Luke 1:37, *The Amplified Bible*).

The winds of life may blow and the waves of life may toss, but they have no power over the Holy Spirit who lives inside us. Jesus taught this great truth on the lake of Gennesaret (the Sea of Galilee). As Jesus and His disciples crossed the lake one evening, a terrible storm came up. "...a furious storm of wind (of hurricane proportions) arose, and the waves kept beating into the boat, so that it was already becoming filled" (Mark 4:37, *The Amplified Bible*).

The disciples were terrified by the furious storm, but Jesus wasn't. In fact, He was so relaxed that He was sound asleep in the back of the boat. When the disciples frantically awakened Him and told Him that they were afraid of drowning, a beautiful event took place. "...he arose, and rebuked the wind, and said unto the sea, *Peace, be still.* And the wind ceased, and there was a great calm. And he said unto them, *Why* are ye so fearful? *how is it* that ye have no faith?" (Mark 4:39-40).

The same great peaceful Lord who caused the wind and the sea to quiet down many years ago lives inside us today. "Jesus Christ *the same* yester-day, and to day, and for ever" (Hebrews 13:8). He doesn't want us to be worried or afraid today any more than He wanted His disciples to be worried and afraid. When the storms of life come at us, He wants us to *"be still,* and *know* that I am God...".

He wants us to face every circumstance in our lives calmly because we know that He is with us and that He can and will take care of everything. Fear and worry show that we *don't* believe that He will. Calmness in the face of adversity indicates that we *do* trust Him.

In order to relax in the face of adversity, we

have to get in tune with our Father and be part of His rhythm. This rhythm causes the tide to come in and go out, the sun to rise and set, and summer, autumn, winter and spring to come and go. The birds pick up His rhythm and some instinctively migrate to the south in the fall. Squirrels instinctively know when to store up nuts for the winter.

The sun, moon, earth and a multitude of other planets all orbit perfectly in God's order. Throughout the universe, many occurrences take place each day based upon God's timing. Fear and anxiety *stop* us from getting into His rhythm. We get into this rhythm only if we do our best and then slow down, calmly trusting in our Lord to guide us effortlessly and smoothly.

If we become overeager and anxious, we lose God's peace. Our Father's peace requires complete trust that He *will* give us the answer in His way and in His time, *not* in our way and in our timing. He wants our tempo to be His tempo and His tempo is always perfect. It is never hurried or rushed.

A quiet, humble, trusting attitude is necessary in order to receive the great abundance of peace that our Father has for us. "...the *meek* shall inherit the earth; and shall *delight* themselves in the *abundance of peace*" (Psalm 37:11). Jesus told us that His meek, humble attitude would bring quietness to our souls. "...*learn of Me;* for I am *gentle* (meek) and *humble* (lowly) in heart, and you *will find rest*—relief, ease and refreshment and recreation and blessed quiet—for your souls" (Matthew 11:29, *The Amplified Bible*).

Pride and peace don't go together. Pride blocks us from receiving the peace of God. Pride puts self first, focuses on self and trusts in self. Our Father's peace is available to us only if we realize how totally dependent we are on *Him*. Humility is an absolute necessity in order to enter into a trusting relationship with the Lord so that we can enjoy the peace that He has given to us.

This peace is not available to hard-headed, prideful, "I'll do it my way" people. It is only available to humble Christians who will constantly yield to the Lord, study and meditate continually in His Word and then live their lives the way that He tells us to live them.

We must give God complete control of our lives, fully realizing that we cannot do anything of real significance by ourselves and that everything we need comes from Him. *"Not that we are sufficient of ourselves* to think *any thing* as of ourselves; but *our sufficiency is of God"* (II Corinthians 3:5).

When we are faced with monumental problems, we shouldn't be upset because we don't believe that we can handle them. Instead, we should glory in our weakness, realizing that this is what enables the Lord's strength to be released in our lives. Paul learned this when, on three different occasions, He went to the Lord and asked for relief from tremendous burdens:

"Three times I called upon the Lord and besought [Him] about this and begged that it might depart from me; but He said to me, *My grace*—My favor and loving-kindness and mercy— are *enough* for you, [that is, sufficient against *any* danger and to enable you to bear the trouble manfully]; *for My strength and power are made perfect—fulfilled and completed and show themselves most effective—in [your] weakness.* Therefore, I will all the more gladly glory in my weaknesses and infirmities, that the strength and power of Christ, the Messiah, may rest—yes, may pitch a tent [over] and dwell—upon me!" (II Corinthians 12:8-9, *The Amplified Bible*).

35

Isn't this wonderful? The strength of our Lord is released in our lives in exact proportion to the acknowledgement of our human weakness. *"...when I am weak* (in human strength), *then am I [truly] strong*—able, powerful in *divine strength"* (II Corinthians 12:10, *The Amplified Bible*).

The world has this backward. The world teaches that peace comes from security in our personal strength and abilities. God's Word says, *"...for by strength shall no man prevail"* (I Samuel 2:9). When we can't get the job done, we need to *admit* our weakness and trust in His strength—*"My flesh and my heart faileth: but God is the strength of my heart, and my portion for ever"* (Psalm 73:26).

We receive the peace of God and all of His other blessings when our strength comes from Him. *"Blessed* is the man *whose strength is in thee..."* (Psalm 84:5). No matter how bad our troubles might seem, God's strength is always available to us. *"God is our refuge and strength, a very present help in trouble"* (Psalm 46:1).

Too many of us react far too strongly to situations that we shouldn't react to. Our Father's strength is more than sufficient, no matter what comes against us. All of us want to receive this strength in our lives, but how many of us know the two specific things that God's Word says are required in order to release His strength in our lives? Time and time again I have asked this basic scriptural question and very few people know the simple answer.

We are given the answer in another verse of Scripture that I often meditate on whenever I'm confronted with problems that seem to be too much for me. *"...in quietness* and in *confidence* shall be your strength..."* (Isaiah 30:15). Our Father's strength is released in our lives in exact proportion to the degree that we are able to, 1) *remain calm and quiet* in the face of seemingly severe problems, and, 2) *trust completely* in Him.

Our Father never intended for us to solve monumental problems with our limited human abilities!! Instead, He wants us to build our faith in Him to the point where we can remain very calm in the face of seemingly insurmountable obstacles because of our great trust and confidence in Him!

Human strength never is sufficient for the major problems of life. Instead of trying to do everything with our strength, we need to remain calm, trusting completely in the Lord, waiting patiently on Him. When we do, He will *renew* our strength. He'll make it *brand new*. He'll give us strength that will enable us to *soar high above our problems.* If we trust in His strength, instead of being tired out, we'll even be able to run without getting weary:

"He giveth power *to the faint;* and to them that have *no might* he increaseth strength. Even the youths shall faint and be weary, and the young men shall utterly fall: but they that *wait upon the Lord* shall *renew their strength;* they shall mount up with wings as *eagles;* they shall *run,* and *not* be weary; and they shall *walk,* and *not* faint" (Isaiah 40:29-31).

We shouldn't focus on our human weaknesses. Instead, we should open our mouths and speak of the Lord's strength. "...let the weak *say,* I am strong..." (Joel 3:10). When the problems seem to be more than we can handle, we should open our mouths and confidently *speak* the promises of strength that are contained in the Word of God. We *release spiritual power* by constantly opening our mouths and boldly speaking our Father's Word. When our words clearly indicate that we *know* that *we can't do it* and that we *know* that the Lord *can and will do it*, this *releases power* in the spiritual realm!

Strength comes from quietness and confidence. Calmness in the face of adversity shows trust in the Lord. Weak people struggle, strain and worry, trying to get the job done through human strength, but strong people admit their weakness and get the job done by trusting completely in the strength of the Lord.

Our Father will never force Himself on us. He gave us freedom of choice. He's looking for us to make the right choice—and that is to remain calm, still and quiet because we know that He is Almighty God and that He is in control. *This* is how we release His strength.

Chapter 5

God's Perfect Peace

God's Word tells us that His "perfect peace" is available to us. No other peace remotely compares with God's perfect peace. It is total, complete and absolute—a beautiful peace that never changes.

I'd like to give another "quiz" to each reader of this book. *Do you know* the two scriptural requirements that are necessary in order to receive God's perfect peace? Time after time I have asked Christians what these two requirements are and, invariably, only a small percentage of the people knew.

The following verse of Scripture tells us exactly how to obtain God's perfect peace in our lives. "Thou wilt keep him in perfect peace, whose mind is *stayed on thee:* because he *trusteth in thee"* (Isaiah 26:3).

Our Father will always do His part if we will do our part. His part is to keep us in perfect peace. Our part is, 1) to keep our minds stayed on Him and, 2) to trust completely in Him. Isn't this exactly the *opposite* of what most of us do when we're faced with a crisis??

Don't our minds remain primarily "stayed" on the *problems* that face us? Don't we turn these problems over and over in our minds, focusing on them almost constantly? Don't most of us worry about whether we can solve these problems? In crisis situations, isn't it true that many of us do exactly the opposite of God's two requirements for perfect peace?

Some of us experience "partial peace." We keep our minds partially on the problem and partially on God. We trust partially in ourselves and partially in God. This is an improvement over doing exactly the opposite to the instructions of Isaiah 26:3, but it leaves us a long way from the perfect peace that we can experience.

Why does Isaiah 26:3 teach us that perfect peace is related to our "minds" when Romans 10:9, Proverbs 23:7 and other verses of Scripture place emphasis on our hearts? The answer is that all spiritual battles are fought in our minds. These battles are fought based upon what we believe in our hearts, but the area they take place in is our minds. Our heartfelt beliefs are our "weapons," but our minds are the "battlefield."

Satan got to Adam and Eve by cunningly seducing and corrupting their *minds*. We must be on guard against this same device. "...even as the serpent beguiled Eve by his cunning, so your *minds* may be corrupted and seduced from wholehearted and sincere and pure devotion to Christ" (II Corinthians 11:3, *The Amplified Bible*).

God wants us to keep our minds stayed on Him because He wants us to be *single-minded at all times*. Christians who aren't single-minded risk the problems that attack people who are double-minded. "...a man of *two minds*—hesitating, dubious, irresolute—[he is] *unstable* and *unreliable* and *uncertain* about everything (he thinks, feels, decides)" (James 1:8, *The Amplified Bible*).

Double-minded Christians are *variable*. One day

they're full of faith—defying the problem that they're faced with, boldly claiming the promises of God, praising Him and thanking Him. Yet, a few days, weeks or months later, these same Christians often are filled with doubt and are very hesitant and wavering.

God's Word warns us about the penalties of being double-minded (offering a half-hearted commitment for trusting God one day and worrying another day). "...ask in faith, *nothing wavering*. For he that wavereth is like a wave of the sea driven with the wind and tossed. For let *not* that man think that he shall receive *any thing* of the Lord. A double minded man is *unstable* in all his ways" (James 1:6-8).

Our Father wants us to look only one way—at Him! No matter what problems come into our lives, He wants us to take our eyes *off* the problem and keep them *on* Him. If we do this, the glorious light of our Lord Jesus Christ will shine in our lives. "...if therefore thine eye be *single*, thy whole body shall be *full of light*" (Matthew 6:22).

God's Word places great emphasis on the importance of being single-minded. However, this is easier said than done. Exactly what must be done in order to become single-minded? *How* do we keep our minds on God at all times regardless of circumstances and regardless of what our emotions tell us?

The answer is that our minds have to be made brand new. They have to be constantly refreshed day after day after day. "...be *constantly renewed* in the spirit of your mind—having a fresh mental and spiritual attitude..."(Eph.4:23, *The Amplified Bible*).

We wouldn't think of trying to feed our bodies on one or two meals a week. Yet, this is exactly what many of us try to do with our minds. The only way

41

to keep our minds "stayed" on God is to renew them each and every day through continual study and meditation in His Word.

If we will pay this price, we'll soon find that constant renewal of our minds will transform us by guiding us into living our lives the way that our Father wants us to live. "...be ye *transformed* by the renewing of your mind, that ye may *prove* what is that good, and acceptable, and perfect *will of God*" (Romans 12:2).

If we'll pay the price of constantly renewing our minds so that we're single-minded and focusing on the Lord at all times, the storms of life *won't* be able to hurt us. Think for a moment about a storm at sea. There is no disturbance in the depth of the ocean. It all takes place on the surface.

The storms of life are exactly the same. God is always at peace. Nothing disturbs Him. It's always quiet deep inside ourselves where the Holy Spirit lives. If we keep our minds constantly on Him, the storms of life that take place outside of us won't be able to get down inside of us. They won't be able to get into our minds and, from there, down into our hearts.

This is why God's Word tells us to cast out disturbing thoughts—to stop them from getting into our minds by keeping *every one* of our thoughts on the Lord at all times. *"Casting down* imaginations, and every high thing that exalteth itself against the knowledge of God, and bringing into captivity *every* thought to the obedience of Christ..." (II Corinthians 10:5).

Satan can't get into a mind that is stayed on God. When he tries to get his thoughts into our minds, we need to cast them out. What does a fisherman do when he "casts" his line out into the water? He *throws* it, doesn't he? That's what we must do with the fearful, worried thoughts that try to get into our minds. We need to *throw them out!*

How do we do this??? We do this by keeping our minds *stayed* upon the Lord—by bringing every one of our thoughts into obedience to the Lord. Scientists tell us that we can have as many as 100,000 thoughts going through our minds every day. God's Word tells us that we *can* bring *every* one of these thoughts into captivity to the obedience of Christ by keeping our minds stayed upon Him.

We need to fix our minds on the Lord constantly-not just in morning and evening prayer and at church functions during the week. We need to focus our minds on the Lord throughout the day, each and every day of our lives. This Christ-centered life will lead us into God's perfect peace!

Instead of focusing on the problems in our lives, we need to look to our Lord. This is where our help will come from. "I will *lift up* mine eyes unto the hills from whence cometh my help. My help cometh from the Lord, which made heaven and earth" (Psalm 121:1-2).

If we focus constantly on the Lord, we won't be moved by the circumstances of life. We'll rejoice constantly deep inside of ourselves because we'll be relaxed and at ease no matter what is going on around us. "I have set the Lord *continually* before me; because He is at my right hand, I shall *not* be moved. Therefore my heart is glad, and my glory [my inner self] *rejoices;* my body too shall rest and confidently dwell in safety" (Psalm 16:8-9, *The Amplified Bible).*

Have you noticed when we're exhausted or when our resistance is down how frightening and out of proportion our problems can become? When we focus constantly on the obstacles, they will always seem to be bigger than they really are. This is when we *must keep our minds on the Lord.*

How do we keep our minds stayed on Him? Go back to the final five words of Isaiah 26:3, "...*because he trusteth in thee.*" These words give us the key. We will be able to keep our minds stayed on the Lord in the midst of severe pressure *only* if we honestly trust Him!

Too often, we place our trust in money, government, human intelligence, human abilities, family members and friends. It isn't wrong to trust in those things at times, but it is definitely wrong to trust in them more than we trust in our Lord. We'll never be able to keep our minds stayed on the Lord *unless* we trust Him *much more* than *any* worldly security.

God is our source. All worldly security is temporary and changing. God is permament. He never changes. This world is changing faster today than ever before and change can create anxiety. We must not allow change to rob us of our peace. God never changes. God's Word never changes. Our peace will only be constant to the degree that we focus on our unchanging Father and His unchanging Word.

The mind that is stayed on the Lord is always calm and poised because our Lord is always calm and poised. Nothing can sway this mind because nothing can sway our Lord. The more our minds are centered upon the source of all peace, the more His peace will be manifested in our lives.

In this chapter we have fully explored the need to keep our minds stayed upon the Lord. In our next chapter, we'll focus in more detail on the one attribute that enables us to keep our minds stayed upon the Lord—complete trust in Him. We'll see how we can build our trust in Him to the point where it is *so* strong that our minds will automatically focus on Him no matter how severe our problems might be.

"We'll only experience the peace of God if we're able to turn away from our intellects and our emotions and, instead, trust Him with simple, childlike trust."

Chapter 6

How Do We Trust In The Lord?

The second part of God's "formula" for perfect peace is to *trust* in Him. Actually, this is the first part because Isaiah 26:3 tells us that the reason we can keep our minds stayed on Him is because we trust completely in Him.

This makes sense—if we knew someone who loved us more than we could comprehend, if we loved that "someone" with every bit of love that we possessed and if we knew that "someone" could be totally and completely trusted to take care of us no matter what happened to us, wouldn't we think about that "someone" constantly? We have that "Someone" and His name is God.

Our heavenly Father loves us more than we can possibly imagine. We should love Him with all our hearts and He can and will take care of us no matter what happens to us. However, this care is not "automatic." We will receive from Him in relation to our faith in Him. "...*According to your faith be it unto you*" (Matthew 9:29).

Complete, absolute, unwavering trust in the Lord will cause us to keep our minds stayed on Him no matter what is happening to us. If we are able to do this, we will experience His beautiful perfect peace regardless of the circumstances that we might be faced with in our lives. The Hebrew word that is translated "trusteth" in Isaiah 26:3 means to "have no fear because of our security." If we trust deeply in the Lord, we believe that He is completely reliable, that we are absolutely secure and we have no fear of *anything* because we know that His power is greater than anything that will ever come against us.

How can we tell if we really trust the Lord? The answer is simple—we just need to think back to the last few times that we were under extreme pressure. How did we react? Did we stay calm in the midst of these problems because of our absolute trust in the Lord? Or, did we allow ourselves to become worried and upset?

In moments of crisis, our reaction is always based upon what we really believe deep down in our hearts. The peace of God will rule in our hearts based upon the amount of His Word that lives in our hearts. The key to trusting Him is to have our hearts filled with His Word. "...Let thine heart *retain* my words..." (Proverbs 4:4). If our lives are controlled by whatever we deeply believe, we should be very careful about what we allow to get deep into our hearts. "Keep thy heart with *all diligence;* for out of it are *the issues of life*" (Proverbs 4:23).

Our Father wants us to fill our hearts constantly with His Word. When a crisis comes up, He wants His Word to be *so* deeply rooted and firmly established in our hearts that we will *automatically* react to what His Word says instead of reacting with fear to the crisis that we are faced with. "...the righteous shall be in *everlasting remembrance.* He *shall not be afraid* of evil tidings: his heart is *fixed,* trusting in the Lord. His heart is *established,* he *shall not be afraid...*" (Psalm 112:6-8).

God's Word is a storehouse. All of His power is

stored in it. His Word is a seed. If we constantly plant this seed in our hearts, we plant more and more of our Father's power deep down inside of us. These spiritual "seeds" feed our spirits just as food feeds our physical bodies. If we need a lot of power, then we need to plant a lot of spiritual seeds in our hearts.

If we do this continually, these seeds will take root and we'll have a very solid spiritual foundation. Our faith will become more and more established. "Have the *roots* [of your being] *firmly and deeply planted* [in Him]—*fixed* and *founded* in Him—being *continually built up* in Him, becoming *increasingly more confirmed and established* in the faith..." (Colossians 2:7, *The Amplified Bible*).

If we fail to pay the price of continually establishing God's Word in our hearts, we won't have deep spiritual roots to sustain us during a crisis. When a crisis comes up, we'll only be able to hold on for a little while. "And have *no root* in themselves, and so *endure but for a time...*" (Mark 4:17).

When our hearts are full of God's Word, we'll keep our peace because a heart full of God's Word can and will overcome anything and everything that Satan can throw at us. "...*the word of God abideth in you*, and *you have overcome the wicked one*" (I John 2:14).

When our hearts are filled with God's Word, we'll delight in living our lives the way that He wants us to live them. "I *delight* to do thy will, O my God; yea, thy law is *within my heart*" (Psalm 40:8). When our hearts are full of God's Word and we begin to comprehend how awesome His promises are, we'll rejoice at the great treasure that He has given to us. "... I *stand in awe* of only your words. I

49

rejoice in your laws like one who finds a *great treasure*" (Psalm 119:161-162, *The Living Bible*).

We need to have more than just *head knowledge* of God's Word. We need to have *heart knowledge* of His awesome promises. Our hearts need to be *so full* of His Word that it *dominates* our souls (our minds, our emotions and our will) in times of crisis. If our hearts aren't filled with God's Word, we'll falter when the going gets tough. If our hearts are filled with His Word, we won't budge one inch!

It is easy to see how much of God's Word is in our hearts. This is clearly indicated by the words that come out of our mouths during a time of crisis. Jesus said that whatever our hearts are filled with will come out of our mouths. "...out of the abundance of the heart the mouth speaketh" (Matthew 12:34). This is especially true when we're faced with severe pressure.

Many of us forfeit the peace that our Lord has given us by the words that we allow to come out of our mouths when we are under stress. We'll never enjoy God's peace unless we learn to control our tongues. Our tongues *cannot* be permanently controlled by will power. "...the human tongue can be tamed by *no* man..." (James 3:8, *The Amplified Bible*).

Our tongues can only be controlled by what we believe in our hearts. If our hearts are full of worry, fear, doubt and discouragement, then a crisis will bring forth words of worry, fear, doubt and discouragement. Spiritual power is released by the words that we speak. Because of this, we should open our mouths several times each day and speak the Word of God. If our hearts are full of the Word of God, our lips will constantly speak His Word. When our words constantly line up with God's Word, we constantly release His spiritual power.

When everything that can go wrong seems to be going wrong, *this is the time* to open our mouths and speak the promises of God one after another, thanking Him and praising Him for His answer to our problems! His beautiful Word will calm us and quiet us if we will speak it calmly and emphatically in the face of adversity.

If we constantly speak God's Word, this will increase our peace. When our ears constantly hear our own lips speaking God's Word, our faith will grow. "...faith cometh by *hearing*, and *hearing* by *the word of God"* (Romans 10:17). It is very important to realize that our faith grows by *hearing* God's Word. It *will* grow when we hear other people speak God's Word, *but our faith will really grow when our ears constantly hear our mouths speaking the Word of God!*

As we fill our minds and hearts with God's Word, our faith will become more and more childlike in nature. Little children are at peace because of their innocent trust. Our Father wants us to trust Him with this same innocent trust.

Jesus told us that the only way to enter into God's kingdom is with childlike trust. "Verily I say unto you, whosoever shall not receive the kingdom of God as a *little child*, he shall *not* enter therein" (Mark 10:15). The kingdom of God is where God's peace is found. Like little children, we need to trust *completely* in and depend *totally* on our heavenly Father. He is all the security that we'll ever need!

Little children don't worry. They trust their fathers completely. Our heavenly Father wants us to face the seemingly complex problems of life with this same innocent, childlike trust in Him.

His Word tells us to set our intellects aside—to stop trying to figure everything out with our rational, logical, carnal minds. He told us that, instead of leaning unto our human understanding, we should trust Him completely, living every area of our lives as His Word tells us to live them, trusting completely in Him to guide us and direct us. "Trust in the Lord with *all* thine heart; and *lean not unto thine own understanding.* In *all* thy ways acknowledge him, and he *shall* direct thy paths" (Proverbs 3:5-6).

For example, suppose someone had been steadily employed throughout their life and they were suddenly laid off. In a difficult time like this, it is very easy for our intellect and our emotions to run wild, thinking about all of the potential problems that we could face. However, God's Word tells us not to react based upon our human understanding. We need to be still and trust completely in Him, trusting that He has a better job available and that He will provide for us in the interim.

When we are faced with difficult problems, how do we handle them? Do we do the best we can and then let go, trusting completely in our Father with beautiful, simple, childlike trust? Or do we worry and fret and manipulate, twist and turn trying to bring about a solution by our own devices? Do we try to analyze everything and figure everything out with our human intelligence which simply is not capable of doing this?

Our Lord wants us to commit our lives totally to Him, trusting completely in Him. If we will do this, He then will bring about the solution (in His way and in His timing). *"Commit* thy way unto the Lord; *trust* also in him; and he *shall* bring it to pass" (Psalm 37:5).

We'll only experience the peace of God if we're able to turn away from our intellects and our emotions and, instead, trust Him with simple, childlike trust. When little children are afraid, it relaxes them when the strong, quiet hands and loving voices of their parents are there to guide and reassure them. This same parental guidance is available to us if we can relax and let go and trust our heavenly Father.

If we really are one with the Lord—if we truly do yield each day completely to Him and if our hearts are continually being filled with more and more of His Word, we can do all things through His strength and His ability. "I have strength for *all things* in Christ Who empowers me—*I am ready for anything and equal to anything through Him* who infuses inner strength into me [that is, I am self-sufficient in Christ's sufficiency]" (Philippians 4:13, *The Amplified Bible*).

This is my favorite verse of Scripture. It has pulled me up through some very difficult times. When I was on the verge of financial bankruptcy and a complete emotional breakdown, I used to repeat the King James version of Philippians 4:13 over and over and over. Many times I used to say this one hundred times in a row. Speaking this verse of Scripture over and over and meditating on it constantly, saved me from complete financial and emotional ruin. What glorious peace we will receive when we *really believe* the promise of Philippians 4:13! How can we possibly be worried and afraid if we honestly believe and trust completely in the glorious promise of this powerful verse of Scripture??

We always have a refuge—a quiet place to retreat to. The Lord is that refuge. He is that quiet place. If we truly do abide in Him, we'll be able to see our problems as they really are—small, temporary problems that can easily be solved by the Eternal One who holds this entire universe in His everlasting arms. "The eternal God is your *refuge* and *dwelling place*, and underneath are the *ever-lasting arms...*" (Deuteronomy 33:27, *The Amplified Bible*).

Our Father has given us a beautiful sanctuary deep down inside of us. This beautiful place cannot be disturbed by any external happening. This is where God lives. It is called "the secret place of the most High." Our Father wants us to live there with Him, totally at peace, trusting completely in Him. "He that *dwelleth* in the secret place of the most High *shall abide under the shadow of the Almighty. I will say of the Lord, He is my refuge* and *my fortress:* my God; *in Him will I trust*" (Psalm 91:1-2).

We have a refuge and a fortress—a place that is so secret that the world can't find it. It is hidden deep down inside of our hearts. Only God's children can find this secret place. Our Father wants us to find this secret place. He wants us to live there every minute of every hour of every day of our lives. This is our real home—our dwelling place— while we are here on this earth. The world says that we live at a certain street address in a certain city or town, but our Father wants us to really live in the secret place of the most High. When we're in His home, we are safe and secure. We can relax. We're at home. We're out of the storm. He protects us. Everything is taken care of.

Many Christians never find this secret place. Some of us find it, but we don't live there permanently. We wander in and out—sometimes living there and trusting in the Lord and other times leaving His dwelling place, venturing out on our own, trusting in our human abilities.

This is wrong. Our Father wants us to abide with Him *permanently*—all day long, every day of our lives. We will enjoy His perfect peace if we

abide continually with Him in His home in our
hearts. He has provided a place of rest for us and
His Word gives us definite, specific instructions on
how to enter into His rest.

"In moments of crisis our reaction is always based on what we really believe deep down in our hearts."

Chapter 7

The Rest Of God

As we have seen, Isaiah 26:3 tells us that the key to perfect peace is complete trust in the Lord. This causes our minds to remain stayed on Him which enables His perfect peace to manifest itself in our lives.

A great deal of the trust that is required comes from knowing how to enter into the rest of God. The Bible has a lot to say about the subject of rest, particularly in the third and fourth chapters of Hebrews. The Greek word that is translated "rest" in these chapters means "to cease"—to stop doing what we're doing and relax.

Peace and rest go together. People say, "I'm going on vacation next week and I'm going to get a nice, peaceful rest." All of us look for a rest from the pressures and tensions of life. Our Father has made a nice, peaceful rest available to us—not just for a short vacation, but for *every day for the remainder of our lives.*

The third and fourth chapters of Hebrews tell about the Israelites in the desert who failed to enter into the rest of God's Promised Land. We should learn from their example because we are told that this same rest is available to us today. "*...there is still awaiting a full and complete Sabbath rest reserved for the [true] people of God*" (Hebrews 4:9,

The Amplified Bible). It's important to note that this isn't a partial, temporary rest. We are told that it is a "full and complete" rest.

Jesus paid the price for our rest. All Christians will experience this beautiful eternal rest when we get to heaven, but it is also available to us now. This rest will be "automatic" when we get to heaven, but it's *not* automatic now. We have to know exactly *how* to enter into it.

Adam and Eve enjoyed a position of complete rest, but they forfeited it by rebelling against God. Jesus restored this rest. As Christians, we don't have to live the tension-filled life of the world! We are invited to participate in the same rest that our Father and our Lord Jesus enjoy. We are invited to rest from our work just as they are resting from their work.

In Hebrews 4:9 we saw a reference to the "Sabbath rest." This refers to the rest that God Himself took after He spent six days creating the earth. On the seventh day, the Sabbath, He rested. "...And God did rest the seventh day from all his works" (Hebrews 4:4).

Why did God rest on the seventh day? Did He rest because He was tired from the tremendous work that He did during the preceding six days? No. God doesn't get tired. He rested because His work was *finished.*

Jesus is resting because His work is finished, too. Just before He died on the cross, "...He said, *It is finished!* and He bowed His head and gave up His spirit" (John 19:30, *The Amplified Bible).* Jesus now sits at the right hand of God, resting with Him. The completed work of Jesus Christ applies to us. The rest that He enjoys is available to us because we are the beneficiaries of His finished work.

God created us so that we need rest after work. This principle is seen throughout the universe. Our bodies need rest each day, so God created sleep for us. Our stomachs need a period of rest each day, so God provided us with a built-in "fast" to rest our digestive systems each night. This is why we call our morning meal "breakfast" because it means "to break a fast."

All human beings follow the cycle of work and then rest...work and then rest...over and over and over. This same cycle applies in the spiritual realm. We wouldn't dream of working twenty-four hours a day without ever resting and we shouldn't do this in the spiritual realm either. Our minds and emotions need a rest. Tense, worried people don't know how to give their minds a rest. They don't know how to get away from the problems in their lives.

Trust is the key to rest. In the spiritual realm, we overcome unrest by trusting in the Lord. Unrest comes naturally. We don't have to spend hours in study and meditation to learn how to be anxious, worried and afraid. Can you imagine someone writing a book *How To Be Worried?* We don't need to learn negative emotions. They come naturally to us.

The first step towards finding this rest is a willingness to stop trying to carry loads that are too heavy for us. Jesus wants us to come to Him with our heavy burdens (financial problems, health problems, family problems, employment problems, etc.) and allow Him to give us rest. "Come to Me, *all* you who *labor* and are *heavy-laden* and *over-burdened,* and *I will cause you to rest*—I will *ease* and *relieve* and *refresh* your souls" (Matthew 11:28, *The Amplified Bible*).

Isn't this great??? Our Lord tells us that we can take our heavy loads to Him and that He will "ease and relieve and refresh" our souls. He said that He wants to carry our heavy loads. He wants to relieve us of our burdens. Unfortunately, many of us don't trust Him enough to let go of the heavy loads that we're trying to carry.

Jesus isn't going to come charging up to us and say, "Get out of the way. This load is too heavy for you to carry. I'm going to carry it for you." He never forces us to do anything. He told us that He's willing to carry our heavy loads for us. The next move is ours!

God gave all of us freedom of choice. If we choose to try and carry the heavy loads by ourselves, then He has no choice but to let us. He did His part by sending His Son to this earth to pay the price for our sins. Jesus offered to carry our burdens. The next move is up to us.

We'll experience the Lord's rest to the exact degree that we are able to come to Him with our burdens, give them to Him, walk away and never look back, trusting completely in Him to carry them just as He said He would. There is no problem that Jesus can't solve. "...the Lord *has given you rest* from your sorrow and pain, and from your trouble and unrest..." (Isaiah 14:3, *The Amplified Bible*). He is with us constantly and He wants to give us rest. "And he said, My presence shall go with thee, and *I will give thee rest*" (Exodus 33:14).

What is it that stops us from trusting the Lord to carry our heavy loads? Millions of God's children fail to enter into His rest for one reason—*unbelief*— "And to whom did He swear that they should *not* enter His rest, but to those who *disobeyed*—who had *not* listened to His word, and who refused to be compliant or be persuaded? So we see that they were *not* able to enter [into His rest] because of their *unwillingness* to *adhere to* and *trust* and *rely*

on God—*unbelief had shut them out"* (Hebrews 3:18-19, *The Amplified Bible).*

Many of us say and think that we believe in Jesus, but we haven't entered into His rest because we haven't paid the price of continual study and meditation in God's Word. It's impossible to obey God's Word unless we pay the price of learning what it says. We have to plant seeds before we can reap a harvest. Our Father will reveal Himself to us if we'll pay the price of continually studying and meditating in His Word. If we won't pay this price, unbelief will stop many of us from entering into the rest that our Lord has provided for us.

Little children don't show doubt in their parents' ability to solve their problems. We shouldn't have any doubts about our Father's ability to solve our problems. How would any human father feel if his little child clearly showed by his words and actions that he didn't trust him?? Can you imagine a two-year-old child saying, "Daddy, do you have enough money so that we can pay the mortgage payment this month?" Our heavenly Father feels the same way when He sees us worrying and straining and struggling with our heavy loads instead of trusting Him.

We must allow Him to be Lord. God will do what He says He will do in His Word. He doesn't want us to get into the position of trying to be God. We're not "passing the buck" when we give our burdens to God. This is what He has requested and it is what He wants us to do. The secret to perfect peace and rest is learning how to carry our burdens until they get heavy and then to *let go* and trust the Lord to carry them from there.

Many Christians don't enter into the rest of God even though they have spent a lot of time studying the Bible. *It isn't enough just to know what God's*

61

Word says. "...the message they heard did *not* benefit them, *because it was not mixed with faith* [that is, with the *leaning of the entire personality* on God in *absolute trust and confidence* in His power, wisdom and goodness] by those who heard it..." (Hebrews 4:2, *The Amplified Bible*).

We will only enter into the rest of God to the degree that we *trust* Him deep down inside of ourselves. "...we who have *believed*—who have adhered to and trusted and relied on God—*do enter into that rest...*" (Hebrews 4:3 *The Amplified Bible*).

God's Word is preached to Christians today just as it was preached to the Israelites in the wilderness. They didn't benefit from God's Word because they didn't believe totally in it. The situation is the same today. We cannot enter into God's rest, unless we believe! We need to *know* what God's Word says and we *also* have to *believe* that He *will* do exactly what His Word says He will do!

Too many of us believe more in our problems than we believe in our Lord's ability to solve these problems. We must not let our unbelief rob us. We need to follow the example of Abraham. "He *staggered not* at the promise of God through unbelief; but was *strong in faith*, giving glory to God; and being *fully persuaded* that, what he had promised, *he was able also to perform*" (Romans 4:20-21).

The Greek word that is translated "persuaded" means "to be assured." How can we do anything except rest if we *truly* have a deep inner assurance that our Father will do exactly what His Word says He will do?? *Why* would we ever struggle and strain, trying to get the job done by ourselves if we really do believe that His magnificent power is available to us???

He has all the answers. He can see many solutions when we can't see any possible solution. He'll take care of everything *if* we'll just let go and trust Him!

"Pride and unbelief stop us from entering into the rest of God which can only be entered into through humility and trust."

Chapter 8

Entering Into
The Rest Of God

In Matthew 11:28, Jesus told us to come to Him with our heavy loads and He would give us rest. Let's examine the next two verses of Scripture carefully in order to receive specific instructions on *how* to enter into God's rest.

Jesus said, "Take my yoke upon you, and learn of me; for I am meek and lowly in heart: and ye shall find rest unto your souls. For my yoke is easy, and my burden is light" (Matthew 11:29-30). What does this mean?

The Greek word that is translated "yoke" means a wooden frame that is used to fit a pair of animals together. *Webster's New World Dictionary* says that a "yoke" is "a wooden frame fitted around the necks of pairs of oxen, etc. for harnessing them together... something that binds, unites or connects...to be joined together or closely united."

Visualize a pair of oxen joined together by a wooden yoke around their necks. They have no freedom of movement. They are locked in place. They are completely controlled by that yoke. They have to do exactly what the person controlling the yoke wants them to do even though that person is much smaller and weaker than they are.

Jesus will take care of our heavy loads *if we will get into His yoke.* Instead of struggling and straining, trying to carry these heavy loads, He wants us to get into His yoke—to *turn control of our lives over to Him.*

In many cases, people struggle and struggle until they finally realize that they can't go any further. In desperation, they cry out to the Lord and ask Him to please do something. This is the point where many people surrender themselves to Jesus and He carefully fits His yoke upon them and handles the problem. However, the Lord wants us to learn to *let go* and to *trust Him* well *before* we reach the point of desperation!

If we will do this, He tells us that we will "learn" from Him. We need to "rest" in His yoke just as oxen rest in their yoke—completely under the control of the person who is leading them. He will lighten our load. He will guide us. Life is much easier and our burdens are much lighter if we get into His yoke and stay there. This is why Jesus said that His yoke is *"easy"* and His burden is *"light."*

How do we get into Jesus' yoke and find rest for our souls? Let's look again at eleven of the words that Jesus said in Matthew 11:29 in order to find the answer. "...learn of me; for I am meek and lowly in heart...". Jesus said that we can enter into this rest *if we are meek and lowly in our hearts, just as He is.*

Jesus was so meek and lowly that He actually said, "...The Son can do *nothing* of himself..." (John 5:19). This refers to Jesus' human nature. In order to identify with mankind, He voluntarily gave up His divine power. He didn't waste effort trying to carry the load by Himself. He knew He couldn't do it, so He let go and trusted God living inside of Him to do the works. "...the Father dwelleth in me, *he doeth the works"* (John 14:10).

We enter into our Lord's rest through *humility*

and *trust*—the humility to know that we *can't* carry the big loads of life and the trust to *believe* that He can and will carry them if we'll just let go and allow Him to carry them. *Pride and unbelief stop us from entering into the rest of God which can only be entered into through humility and trust.* Whether we realize it or not, when we struggle and strain and worry, trying to carry the loads by ourselves, we're really saying, "I don't trust the Lord to carry this load. I guess I'm going to have to try and carry it by myself."

We may think we trust the Lord, but if we *really* did trust Him, *why* would we be struggling to carry the heavy loads of life ourselves??? We enter into His rest only to the degree that we humbly admit that we *can't* do it and quietly and humbly trust Him to do it for us.

We can't rest if we're convinced that we've got to get the job done with our human abilities. Self-confidence isn't the answer. Self-confidence is the world's way. *"Christ-confidence"* is God's way. We cannot enter into God's rest without meekly acknowledging our own inadequacy and humbly admitting our complete dependence upon the Lord.

It's so clear! We can only enter into God's rest to the degree that we *stop trying to do it all by ourselves.* We need to relax just as God relaxed when He entered into His rest. We need to stop fretting and rest quietly and confidently and patiently in the Lord. *"Rest in the Lord, and wait patiently for him: fret not thyself..."* (Psalm 37:7).

Many of our problems come because we try to do the Lord's job for Him! How it must hurt the Lord to see so many of us ignoring His immense power as we struggle, strain, hurry and worry, trying to carry life's heavy loads with our own strength and ability.

Much of our work and sweat and striving to get things done with our human abilities is meaningless. All of this doesn't count for anything in the spiritual realm. We're just chasing after the wind. "...as I looked at everything I had tried, *it was all so useless, a chasing of the wind, and there was nothing really worthwhile anywhere*" (Ecclesiastes 2:11, *The Living Bible*).

The Lord can do a much better job of running our lives than we can. We simply can't understand the principles of the spiritual realm. "Man's goings are of the Lord; *how can a man then understand his own way?*" (Proverbs 20:24). Our Lord doesn't want us in control. "...the way of man is *not* in himself: it is *not* in man that walketh to direct his steps" (Jeremiah 10:23).

We release the Lord's power by humbling ourselves before Him and trusting in Him. We block His power when we try to do everything by ourselves. If we really trust the Lord, we'll stay calm in the face of adversity. We won't get restless and tense. He can easily handle the problems that seem totally impossible to us. He will do exactly what His Word says He will do. "For with God *nothing is ever impossible,* and *no* word from God shall be *without power* or *impossible* of fulfillment" (Luke 1:37, *The Amplified Bible*).

Hebrews 4:10 tells us that, in order to enter into God's rest, we have to *cease* from our own works—to stop trying to do it all ourselves. Hebrews 4:11 then goes on to say, "Let us *labour* therefore to enter into that rest, lest any man fall after the same example of unbelief." At first glance, this sounds contradictory. Verse 10 says that we enter into God's rest by "ceasing" from our own work and then verse 11 tells us that we need to "labour" to enter into God's rest. What does this mean?

We find the answer by looking up the meaning of the Greek word that is translated "labour." The same word *spoudazo* that is translated "labour" in Hebrews 4:11 is translated to mean "study" in II Timothy 2:15—"Study to shew thyself approved unto God, a workman that needeth not to be ashamed, rightly dividing the word of truth."

We enter into God's rest by working hard at studying His Word. Hebrews 4:12 describes the awesome power of God's Word: "For the word of God is quick, and powerful, and sharper than any two-edged sword, piercing even to the dividing asunder of soul and spirit, and of the joints and marrow, and is a discerner of the thoughts and intents of the heart" (Hebrews 4:12).

This tells us that God's Word is so powerful and supernatural that it is *sharper* than the sharpest sword. It is so strong that it can actually *cut deeply* into the dividing line between our souls and our spirits, showing us *exactly what we're like* deep down inside of ourselves.

The next verse tells us that God knows everything about every one of us. We can't hide a single thing from Him. "Neither is there *any* creature that is not manifest in his sight: but *all things* are naked and opened unto the eyes of him with whom we have to do" (Hebrews 4:13). Our Father knows everything we think, everything we say and everything we do. His Word is like a mirror showing us what we're really like.

If we want to enter into the rest of God, we have to study diligently in order to learn His way of doing things. If we don't do this, we'll constantly make mistakes and we'll easily be led astray. This stops us from entering into His rest. "...*They always err and are led astray in their hearts, and they have not perceived or recognized My ways and become*

69

progressively better and more experimentally and intimately acquainted with them. Accordingly I swore in My wrath and indignation, they shall *not* enter into My rest" (Hebrews 3:10-11, *The Amplified Bible*).

God became angry with the Israelites because they refused to pay the price of progressively learning more and more about His ways by constantly studying His Word. We can't skim through God's Word. We must absorb it and learn gradually, one phrase at a time and one line at a time, one precept after another until finally we are able to enter into His rest. "For precept must be upon precept, precept upon precept; line upon line, line upon line; here a little, and there a little: for with stammering lips and another tongue will he speak to this people. To whom he said, *This is the rest wherewith ye may cause the weary to rest; and this is the refreshing:* yet they would *not* hear" (Isaiah 28:10-12).

God tried to tell the Israelites that they needed to study His Word, learning one line at a time, one precept after another in order to enter into His rest, but they wouldn't listen. The same thing is happening today. Large numbers of Christians fail to enter into the rest that our Father has provided for us because many of us simply won't "labor"—we won't work hard at studying His Word and learning His ways.

God's Word is the spiritual food that causes our faith to grow. When we're faced with severe adversity in our lives, we'll only be able to remain calm and enter into His rest if we *disregard our way* of doing things because we have learned and obeyed our Father's laws that are spelled out in His Word. "The Lord knows the thoughts of man, that they are *vain, empty* and *futile*—only a breath.

Blessed—happy, fortunate [to be envied]—is the man whom You discipline and instruct, O Lord, and *teach out of Your law;* that You may give him power to *hold himself calm* in the days of adversity..." (Psalm 94:11-13, *The Amplified Bible*).

How do we enter into a calm, restful state in the midst of adversity? It's just as clear as it can be—we do this by learning God's laws so that we do everything His way instead of the vain, empty, futile ways that men try to do things. We can and will enter into the rest of God to the exact degree that we, (a) *know* what His Word says, and, (b) *deeply believe* that He *will* do exactly what His Word says that He will do.

Our Lord has given us a clear path to follow. If we follow His instructions, we will find the rest that we crave. "Thus says the Lord, Stand by the roads and *look, and ask for the eternal paths*, where is the good, old way; then *walk in it, and you will find rest for your souls...*" (Jeremiah 6:16, *The Amplified Bible*).

*"Peace, in its truest sense, means
"oneness with God."*

Chapter 9

Peace Instead Of Worry

God's Word tells us that a peace is available to us that is *so great that we cannot understand it* with our limited human understanding. We cannot understand this peace because it rests completely on the truth of God's Word. If we follow the specific directions that are given to us, we will be able to receive this supernatural peace of God in our lives.

The Apostle Paul knew what he was talking about when he wrote about the peace of God that passes all understanding. His explanation of this peace wasn't written in a nice, comfortable room. He wrote the magnificent words of Philippians 4:6-7 while being held in a Roman jail. In these two verses of Scripture, Paul tells us the one thing that robs us of God's peace and the two things that we must do in order to receive the peace of God which passes all understanding.

The Living Bible clearly shows us what robs us of this peace and what we need to do in order to receive this peace. Let's look at these two verses of Scripture in their entirety and then we will go through them in careful detail. *"Don't worry about anything;* instead, *pray about everything;* tell God your needs and don't forget to *thank Him for His answers.* If you do this *you will experience God's peace, which is far more wonderful than the human mind can understand.* His peace will keep your thoughts and your hearts *quiet and at rest* as you trust in Christ Jesus" (Philippians 4:6-7, *The Living Bible*).

First, let's carefully consider the first four words of Philippians 4:6. "Don't worry about anything...". If you look at Philippians 4:6 in the King James version of the Bible, you'll see that it starts with the words "Be careful for nothing...". Many people don't understand this and the reason is that the word "careful" that was used when the King James version was written does not mean the same as it does today. This word actually means "full of care" and this is why most of the subsequent translations of the Bible clearly indicate that we should never be "full of care" or worried about anything.

Unfortunately, many people regularly violate these four words of instruction from God's Word. The fact is that most of us, unless we were brought up in a strong, Bible-believing, Christian environment, have probably been "programmed" with a considerable amount of worry ever since our childhood.

There is a great deal of worry in the world today and one reason for this is the powerful effect of the news media. Our newspapers, magazines, radios and television sets pour out a steady diet of food for anxiety—a slumping economy, unemployment, trouble overseas, plane, train and automobile crashes, murders, rapes, robberies and much more.

In addition, many of us even project our worry into the weather forecast, "How bad is the weather going to be?", and then into the sports news, "Why isn't our home team winning?" When we add all of this to the personal problems between husbands and wives, difficulties with children, drugs, alcohol and other domestic problems, is it any wonder that so many people are worried?

Worry is one of the major causes of health problems. It ages our bodies. It causes ulcers and high blood pressure. It causes sleepless nights. It eats away at our minds and drains us dry emotionally. *Worry is suicide on the installment plan.*

Worry doesn't serve any good purpose. There is nothing positive about worry. It doesn't help us in the least. All that it can do is hurt us. Every aspect of worry is negative, yet millions of people do it on a regular basis. *Nowhere* in the Bible do we find instructions telling us to worry. God's Word *never* advocates tension, confusion, hurry and worry. Instead, it speaks over and over about calmness, peace, contentment and trust. God's Word specifically tells us *not to worry.*

Jesus, in His Sermon on the Mount, said, "*...stop being perpetually uneasy (anxious and worried)* about your life..." (Matthew 6:25, *The Amplified Bible).* He told us that worry is useless. "And which of you by worrying and being anxious can add one unit of measure [cubit] to his stature or to the span of his life?" (Matthew 6:27, *The Amplified Bible).*

We worry because we don't know the promises of God or, if we do, we don't trust them. *If* we have paid the price of learning a large number of God's promises and *if* we deeply believe that our Father will do exactly what His Word says He will do, *why would we ever worry???*

Whether we realize it or not, when we worry we give more power to the problem than we do to our Father who can solve every problem. Worry leads us towards problems and away from God. Peace does the opposite. Peace leads us away from problems and towards God. Peace, in its truest sense, means *"oneness with God."* Worry tries to destroy our oneness with God by getting us to take our eyes off Him.

God's Word tells us that He wants us *"Looking unto Jesus* the author and finisher of our faith..." (Hebrews 12:2). Jesus is the source of all faith. He is greater than any problem we will ever experience. When we accepted Him as our Saviour, our Father gave each of us a specific amount of faith. "...God hath dealt to every man *the measure of faith"* (Romans 12:3). If we'll *keep our eyes on Jesus, He will "finish" our faith*—He'll cause it to grow and grow and grow.

It is a fact that worry is actually a sin. *"...whatsoever is not of faith is sin"* (Romans 14:23). I have discussed these seven words with many people who are chronic worriers and this always makes them feel guilty. Nevertheless, this is exactly what God's Word says. Over and over His Word tells us not to be afraid and not to worry. When we disboey these instructions, we clearly sin.

We don't have to feel guilty and condemned because of this. If we go to our Father and admit our sin and ask for forgiveness, He will forgive us. He understands that we worry. He will forgive us for worrying. However, if we are going to learn how to manifest His supernatural peace in our lives, we must learn how to overcome worry.

Worry is caused by *insecurity*. We have the greatest security this universe has ever known— God's Word, which contains thousands of promises from our Father. Worry comes from allowing our old, proud, carnal, lower nature to dominate our new, humble recreated, spiritual nature. In order to stop worrying, our old, self-oriented nature must be brought under the control of our renewed, selfless new nature.

"...God sets Himself *against the proud*—the insolent, the overbearing, the disdainful, the presumptuous, the boastful, and opposes, frustrates and defeats them—but *gives grace (favor, blessing) to the humble.* Therefore *humble yourselves* (demote, lower yourselves in your own estimation) under the mighty hand of God, that in due time He may exalt you. *Casting the whole of your care—all* your anxieties, *all* your worries, *all* your concerns, *once and for all—on Him...*" (I Peter 5:5-7, *The Amplified Bible).*

We are instructed to cast *all* of our anxieties and worries on God. However, *what* is it that stops many of us from casting all of these negative emotions on Him? The answer is that we must *humble ourselves* under the mighty hand of God *before* we are able to cast our cares on Him. It is impossible to trust God without first of all humbling ourselves before Him.

One form of pride is the insistence that we have to take care of our own problems. If we fail to humble ourselves before God, thus enabling us to give Him our problems, we put ourselves in a position where we actually force Him to resist us. God doesn't want us worrying about anything. He wants us to cast every bit of anxiety on Him.

Many of us worry about the future. God doesn't want us worrying about the future. He is in control of the future. This is His domain and we should leave it to Him. He wants us to live one day at a time, trusting Him for each day.

Most of the things that we worry about never happen. We shouldn't borrow trouble in advance. God wants us to do the best we can each day and then let go, letting Him take it from there. Jesus told us to live our lives one day at a time. *"...don't be anxious* about tomorrow. God *will* take care of your tomorrow too. *Live one day at a time"* (Matthew 6:34, *The Living Bible).*

If we can trust Jesus Christ for our eternal life, we can trust Him with our daily problems! How do we do this? We do this by constantly drawing closer to Him. *"...just as you trusted Christ to save you, trust Him, too, for each day's problems; live in vital union with Him"* (Colosians 2:6, *The Living Bible).*

None of us know what tomorrow holds, but we *do* know *Who* holds tomorrow! If, instead of worrying, we trust completely in Him, living calmly, one day at a time, He will take care of everything.

We can't have God's peace and still worry. The two don't go together. Elimination of worry is the first part of God's "formula" for the peace that passes all understanding. In our next chapter we'll see exactly what the Lord wants us to do instead of worrying.

Chapter 10

How To Overcome Worry

Philippians 4:6 tells us that we shouldn't worry about anything. For many of us this is much easier said than done. *How* do we stop ourselves from worrying? Let's look again at Philippians 4:6-7 for the answer:

"Don't worry about anything; *instead, pray about everything;* tell God your *needs* and don't forget to *thank Him for His answers.* If you *do this* you *will* experience God's peace, which is *far more wonderful* than the human mind can *understand.* His peace *will* keep your thoughts and your hearts *quiet* and *at rest* as you trust in Christ Jesus" (Philippians 4:6-7, *The Living Bible).*

We see that God's Word tells us that, instead of worrying, we should take *every* need to Him in prayer. Then we should *thank Him* for His answers. In all honesty, how many people really do this?? Most of us do just the opposite. Instead of immediately taking every problem to the Lord in prayer and thanking Him for His answer, most of us struggle with the problem and worry about it. After we struggle and worry, *then* many of us go to the Lord in prayer.

Too often prayer is our *last resort* instead of our *first resort.* God's Word tells us that we should go *immediately* to the Lord with every problem. We should always seek Him *first.* Our Father wants us to develop ourselves spiritually so that we'll automatically go to Him in prayer instead of being ruled by our emotions.

It doesn't take any skill to worry. This comes naturally and it's easy to do. However, it takes spiritual maturity to look calmly at every crisis and, without any negative emotional reactions, turn to the Lord and bring every problem to Him in prayer. *This is the way to overcome worry.* We should *refuse* to dwell on problems. Whenever a problem comes up in our lives, we should *immediately* take it to the Lord.

Our prayers should be definite, specific requests. They should be positive prayers of faith based upon specific promises in God's Word. Our Father doesn't want us to pray negatively. He doesn't want us to beg. Negative, doubting, begging prayers show our doubts and anxieties.

Our Father isn't going to answer prayers that are against His will. He isn't some kind of a "bellhop" just waiting to do anything that we tell Him to do. Some faith teachers emphasize a verse of Scripture which says "And *all things, whatsoever* ye shall ask in prayer, believing, ye *shall* receive" (Matthew 21:22), and they say that God will answer every prayer if our faith is strong enough.

However, God's Word also says, "...you do ask [God for them] and yet *fail to receive*, because you ask with *wrong purpose and evil, selfish motives...*" (James 4:3, *The Amplified Bible*). We can ask with tremendous faith, but if our prayers are selfish and not in line with God's will for our lives, we will *not* receive a positive response.

How can we be *sure* that our prayers are in accordance with God's will? This is achieved by always keeping God in *first place* in our lives. If we really do keep God first in every area of our lives, month after month and year after year, it is much more likely that our lives will be surrendered to His will for us and that our prayers *will* be in line with His will.

Another way of assuring that our prayers are based upon God's will is to continually study and meditate in His Word. God's Word and His will are one and the same. The more we study His Word, the *better* we'll know His will. If we constantly seek to put Him first in our lives, and if our humble, trusting prayers are based solidly upon His Word, then it is reasonable to believe that we are praying according to His will.

God's Word has some very interesting things to say about prayers that are made according to His will. We are told, 1) that we will *know* that He *hears* our prayers and, 2) that we will *know* that we *have an answer* to the requests that we bring to Him. "And this is the confidence that we have in him, that, if we ask *any thing according to his will,* he *heareth* us: and if we *know* that he hear us, whatsoever we ask, we *know* that we *have* the petitions that we desired of him" (I John 5:14-15).

These are powerful words! *Instead of worrying* about the problems in our lives, we should go to our Father with specific requests regarding these problems. His Word says that if these requests are according to His will, we will know for certain that He hears us. We also know that we have His answer to our requests.

This is hard for some people to believe. It's too simple. We think, "It must be more complicated than this." No, it isn't! Our Father is looking for childlike trust. He wants us to know that, as long as we are asking according to His will, that He *will* grant our requests.

If we really do believe this, then we'd never worry, would we??? As long as our requests to God are made according to His will, we'd pray with strong, unwavering faith, knowing that He will answer just as His Word says that He will. This is where the part about "giving thanks" comes in. If, deep down in our hearts, we *really* believe that God will answer, then *we will thank Him as we pray.* Let me give you an example of this that I often have used in explaining prayer and thanksgiving.

Think of someone who loves you and trusts you. Imagine that this person lives in another city and that you called them up and said, "I sent you $100 in the mail today." Would that person say, "I'll wait to see if the post office delivers it and then I'll wait to see if your check clears my bank. When I have the money in my hand, *then* I'll thank you."?

That sounds pretty ridiculous, doesn't it? If that person *trusted you,* he or she would *thank you immediately* for sending the money. If you said that you had sent it, this would be *all they needed to know. Why should it be any different with our Father in heaven?* If we go to Him in prayer with unwavering, childlike trust, bringing specific petitions to Him that we know are in His will, *why wouldn't we thank Him when we bring our requests to Him?* Do we have to wait until He gives us an answer before we thank Him? Of course we don't!

As long as our prayers are in the will of God, we should give thanks immediately because I John 5:15 tells us that we *"know"* that we have *"whatsoever we ask." When we refuse* to worry, doubt and complain and, *instead,* go to the Lord in humble, trusting prayer and thank Him for this answer, *our*

Lord will give us His glorious peace—a peace that is so great that we can't understand it!

A constant attitude of thanksgiving reaches out into the spiritual realm and brings us the answer that we need to receive. When we refuse to worry and, instead go calmly to the Lord in prayer, thanking Him for His answer, *we rise above the problems in our lives.* We show that we are on a higher spiritual level than the problems that are trying to get at us and we refuse to sink to their level. The peace of God that passes all understanding manifests itself in the midst of a problem—at a time when, by the world's standards, we shouldn't have any peace whatsoever. *This is why it passes all understanding.*

The next verse of Scripture tells us what we need to do in order to manifest this peace in our lives. We should refuse to worry and think of negative things. Instead, our Lord wants us to focus constantly on His truth, reverence, honor, justice, purity, loveliness, kindness and grace. "...whatever is true, whatever is worthy of reverence and is honorable and seemly, whatever is just, whatever is pure, whatever is lovely and lovable, whatever is kind and winsome and gracious, if there is any virtue and excellence, if there is anything worthy of praise, *think on and weigh and take account of these things—fix your minds on them*" (Philippians 4:8, *The Amplified Bible*).

This is how we receive the peace of God which passes all understanding. We should *refuse* to worry and think of negative things. *Instead,* our Lord wants us to focus constantly on His truth, reverence, honor, justice, purity, loveliness, kindness and grace.

If we refuse to worry but, instead, pray to our Lord with faith and thanksgiving, His peace will actually "*...garrison and mount guard over your hearts and minds in Christ Jesus*" (Philippians 4:7, *The Amplified Bible)*. God's magnificent peace will fortify us and *take control* of our hearts and minds. His peace will *dominate* our hearts. His peace will *dominate* our minds.

We decide whether we're going to let the peace ·of God take charge. We do this by the way that we react to severe pressure. If we refuse to worry and, instead, take everything to our Lord in prayer, thanking Him for the answer and focusing entirely on Him instead of the problem, these words and actions *release His supernatural peace* so that it will *rule* our minds and hearts and *carry us through* the difficult times in our lives.

We should pray constantly. We should thank the Lord constantly. "Pray *without ceasing. In every thing give thanks:* for this *is* the will of God in Christ Jesus concerning you" (I Thessalonians 5:17-18). This is our Father's will. He wants us to take *every* problem to Him in prayer. He wants us to pray *constantly* throughout the day. Each time that we pray, He wants us to *thank* Him for the answer that we *know* we will receive.

This is our part. God will always do His part. He will release His supernatural peace to us if we disregard our emotions and, instead, carefully follow the instructions that He has given us in Philippians 4:6-8.

Chapter 11

God's Peace Lives Inside Of Us

One of the greatest sources of deep inner peace
is the tremendous knowledge that God Himself
lives inside of us. "One God and Father of all, who
is above all, and through all, and *in you all*"
(Ephesians 4:6). Jesus Christ lives inside of us.
"...Jesus Christ is *in you...*" (II Corinthians 13:5).
The Holy Spirit lives inside of us. "...the Holy Ghost
which is *in you...*" (I Corinthians 6:19).

God and Jesus are seated next to each other in
heaven. Yet, at the same time, they also live inside
of every Christian. "...in Christ you too are *filled
with the Godhead:* Father, Son and Holy Spirit, and
reach full spiritual stature..." (Colossians 2:10, *The
Amplified Bible*).

The same God who created everything in the
entire universe abides in us. He is ready, willing
and able to strengthen us in every area of our lives.
"...*out of His glorious, unlimited resources He will
give you the mighty inner strengthening of His Holy
Spirit*" (Ephesians 3:16, *The Living Bible*).

If we *really do* comprehend Who makes His
home in us, *how can we ever* allow ourselves to get
"uptight" about what is going on around us?? No
matter what problems come against us in the
world, we can overcome them if we know how to

release the awesome power that is inside of us. "Ye are of God, little children, and *have overcome them:* because *greater* is he that is *in you*, than he that is in the world" (I John 4:4).

Why would we ever be afraid of anything if we truly know that our Lord is always with us?? "...Be *strong* and of a *good courage;* be *not afraid*, neither be thou *dismayed:* for the Lord thy God *is with thee whithersoever thou goest"* (Joshua 1:9).

When we truly realize these facts, we have the safety and security that the whole world is searching for. Wherever we go, the calm, quiet power of our Father goes with us. He will hold our hands just as a father on earth holds his child's hand. He is always there to give us the advice that we need. "...I am *continually with You; You do hold my right hand.* You will *guide me* with Your counsel..." (Psalm 73:23-24, *The Amplified Bible).*

The greatest power in the world is not nuclear power. There is a greater power—the Power Who was able to raise Jesus Christ from the dead. This *same* power lives inside of us. "...the Spirit of God, who raised up Jesus from the dead, *lives in you...*" (Romans 8:11, *The Living Bible).* If we *really* believe this, *we won't ever be afraid of anything!!*

No matter how big our problems might seem to us, they're not big to Him. If He was able to create heaven and earth, why should our problems be difficult for Him? "Ah Lord God! behold, thou hast made the heaven and the earth by thy great power and stretched out arm, and there is *nothing* too hard for thee..." (Jeremiah 32:17). Nothing is impossible for our Constant Companion. "...With men it is impossible, but *not with God:* for with God *all* things are possible" (Mark 10:27).

God Himself dwells within us and He can do much more than we would ever dream of asking

Him to do. We can't even begin to comprehend His mighty power. "Now glory be to God who by His mighty power at work within us is able to do *far more than we would ever dare to ask or even dream of—infinitely beyond our highest prayers, desires, thoughts, or hopes*" (Ephesians 3:20, *The Living Bible*).

His peace belongs to us in exact proportion to our ability to *turn away from* all that goes on around us and, *instead*, turn to His magnificent Presence living within us. His power is released in proportion to our calmness and faith in the face of adversity.

No matter what we are faced with, we should remain calm. God is there. No matter how bad things are on the outside, all is well on the inside. When we face difficult problems, the Holy Spirit stands firm. He doesn't waver in the least. He remains perfectly calm and supremely confident in the face of every problem. No matter how severe the problem is, He knows that He can handle it easily.

He is not the variable. The problem is not the variable. They are the two constants. *The variable is us.* What will we identify with? Will we give up our peace by identifying with the *problem?* Or, will we keep this peace by identifying with the *solution*— by remaining absolutely calm because we trust totally and completely in the Holy Spirit who lives inside of us?

We must let Him be God! We must accept the fact that we are His people and stop trying to be God ourselves. "...for ye are the temple of the living God; as God hath said, I will dwell in them, and walk in them; and *I will be their God, and they shall be my people*" (II Corinthians 6:16).

No matter how bad the storms of life might be, there is perfect peace and calmness inside of us. We see a good example of this in the "eye" of a hurricane. In the center of every hurricane there is a calm, quiet area which is called the "eye." No matter how strong the force of that hurricane might be, it is perfectly calm in the center.

When pilots are caught in a hurricane, they sometimes try to fly through it and get into the safety of its "eye." Our situation is very similar. When we are caught in the storms of life, we need to turn to the Holy Spirit within us. His calmness and peace are not affected in the least by the storms of life that are raging on the outside.

His peace is not dependent upon what is happening in the world. His perfect peace existed before this world existed and it will remain after this world has ceased to exist. *The more we identify with Him, the less we'll be disturbed by external circumstances.* We will know that our inner resources are too strong for anything in this world to overcome.

Can you imagine God making excuses? Can you imagine God quitting? When we make excuses or quit, we have stopped trusting in the Lord! He doesn't need any excuses. He'll never quit. He has already won a total victory.

The Spirit of victory lives inside of us. He never complains. He never gives up. He has won a total victory and His victory is our victory. His peace flows inside of us. No matter how tired or hot or weary we might be, His river of peace is there to refresh us.

In this chapter we have explained some absolutely immense truths about Who lives inside of us. I urge each reader to go back over this chapter and to spend a great deal of time meditating on the fact that the Holy Spirit actually dwells within us. Turn these verses of Scripture over and over in your mind. Repeat them constantly with your mouth. Great power will be released by meditating on these wonderful truths.

Don't just read this chapter. Please spend a great deal of time meditating on it. You will be greatly rewarded for the time that you spend.

"We can't fill anything...unless it is empty."

Chapter 12

Releasing The Peace That Is Inside Of Us

We have established that God lives inside of us in the form of the Holy Spirit, that He is always with us and that nothing is too difficult for Him. Knowledge of these facts should give us deep inner peace, but the truth is that many Christians know that God's Word says these things, yet still miss out on the deep inner peace that can only be received from the Holy Spirit.

All of the concepts of deep inner peace are tied to our ability to surrender to the power of the Holy Spirit. *How*, specifically, do we surrender to Him in order to find the deep inner peace that only He can provide?

This process starts with spiritual rebirth. When we believe in our hearts in eternal salvation through Jesus Christ and confess this belief with our mouths we are reborn spiritually (Romans 10:9-10). This spiritual rebirth opens the doors for us to enter into the kingdom of God. Jesus said, "...Verily, verily, I say unto thee, Except a man be born again, he *cannot* see the kingdom of God" (John 3:3).

How do we find this kingdom? We won't find it through our senses. We can't see it. "...The kingdom of God cometh *not* with observation" (Luke 17:20).

The reason we can't see God's kingdom is because it is *inside* of us. "...the kingdom of God is *within you*" (Luke 12:21). We must not neglect the tremendous gift that God has put inside of us. *"Neglect not* the gift that is in thee..." (I Timothy 4:14).

We enter into God's kingdom through spiritual rebirth by surrendering our lives to Jesus Christ as our Saviour. Unfortunately, many Christians stop there! Jesus wants to be more than our Saviour. He also wants to be our Lord! He lives inside of us in the form of the Holy Spirit and He also wants to live His life through us. He wants us to let Him be Lord and Master over *every* aspect of our lives. We cannot receive His peace unless we willingly allow Him to control our lives.

His entire kingdom lives inside of us and we'll open its doors when we let go and willingly allow the Holy Spirit—the living Christ inside of us—to control our lives. Like any other gift, the gift of the Holy Spirit can remain unused. If someone gives us a gift, we can use it. We also can decide to leave it sitting in a box, unused, and therefore limit its effectiveness. Many Christians are confused about the Holy Spirit so they tend to ignore Him altogether.

There is quite a bit of disagreement among Christians as to exactly how we receive the fullness of the Holy Spirit. I believe that we should simply realize that our Father wants us to have the fullness of the Spirit and that He is willing to give this to us if we'll do our part.

First of all, we need to *ask* Him. "...how much more shall your heavenly Father give the Holy Spirit *to them that ask him?"* (Luke 11:13). We receive the Holy Spirit by faith. He is there to help us solve every problem to the exact degree that we believe He is. *"...by our faith*—the Holy Spirit helps us with our daily problems..." (Romans 8:26, *The Living Bible*).

God's Word tells us that He wants us to "...*be filled* with the Spirit..." (Ephesians 5:18). Being filled with the Holy Spirit isn't automatic. God will fill us if we'll do our part. What is our part? Our job is to *empty ourselves*. We can't fill anything—our gasoline tanks, a water glass, ourselves, etc.—unless it is *empty*.

The Holy Spirit can only fill us to the degree that we empty ourselves of "self"—our desires, wants and goals and, instead, willingly yield our lives to His will for our lives. "...let your hearts *be filled with God alone* to make them pure and true to Him" (James 4:8, *The Living Bible*).

We can be filled with the Holy Spirit only if we realize how weak we really are and how badly we need to be filled. Proud, self-centered people cannot be filled with the Holy Spirit. Humble, God-centered people are the ones who are open to the in-filling of the Holy Spirit.

The Spirit-filled life is a beautiful life. In the world, people search for such a life through Satan's substitutes of alcohol, drugs and various forms of worldly pleasure. We can obtain what they are looking for and much more without the awful penalties of alcohol and drugs. "...*Do not get drunk with wine, for that is debauchery; but ever be filled and stimulated with the Holy Spirit*" (Ephesians 5:18, *The Amplified Bible*).

Webster's New World Dictionary tells us that "debauchery" means "extreme indulgence of one's appetite, especially for sensual pleasure." The dictionary also says that "debauch" means "to separate...to lead astray." Alcohol, drugs and other temporary forms of pleasure are not the answer. They separate us from God. They lead us astray. At best, they produce only a temporary "high" and repeated use inevitably leads to severe aftereffects.

Instead of getting "drunk with wine," Ephesians 5:18 tells us that we should be filled with the Holy Spirit. As we willingly allow Him to control our lives we'll experience a euphoria that is much greater than any "high" that can be produced by alcohol or drugs. Spirit-filled Christians are full of joy and peace. They just "bubble" over. "May the God of your hope *so fill you with all joy and peace in believing*—through the experience of your faith— that by the power of the Holy Spirit you may *abound and be overflowing (bubbling over) with hope...*" (Romans 15:13, *The Amplified Bible*).

The "high" that the world searches for can only be experienced through yielding our lives to the Holy Spirit. However, being filled with the Holy Spirit is not a one-time occurrence. This process needs to be *repeated* each day of our lives. A great man of God, Rev. Dwight Moody, once said, "A great many think because they have been filled once, they are going to be filled for all time after. My friends, we are leaky vessels and have to keep right under the fountain all the time in order to keep full."

Jesus said, "...If any man will come after me, let him *deny himself*, and take up his cross *daily*, and follow me" (Luke 9:23). Every morning the very first thing that I do after waking up is to say something like this: "Dear Lord, thank you for the good night's sleep. Thank you for this great new day. I rejoice in it. I yield this day totally and completely to your Holy Spirit within me.

"Great Holy Spirit, please take charge of every area of my life throughout this day. I willingly and gladly surrender control of my life to you. Please anoint me and guide me throughout this day.

Please use me in any way that you choose to use me. I surrender every aspect of this day to you. I pray believing in Jesus' Name and I thank you for taking charge of my life today and filling me with yourself as you live your great life through me."

Our Father in heaven wants us to *ask* Him each day to fill us with the Holy Spirit and to *believe* that He will do this! If we really will give up control of our daily lives and, by faith, allow the Holy Spirit to take over, we will "come alive" in the spiritual realm. The peace of the Holy Spirit will be manifested in our lives. "Those who let themselves be controlled by their lower natures live *only to please themselves*, but those who follow after the Holy Spirit find themselves doing those things that *please God*. Following after the Holy Spirit leads to *life* and *peace*, but following after the old nature leads to death..." (Romans 8:5-6, *The Living Bible).*

If, after asking God to fill us with the Holy Spirit, we find ourselves at any point during the day slipping up and taking control of our lives, we should immediately go to the Lord in prayer. We should admit our error and ask His forgiveness and rededicate control of the rest of the day to the Holy Spirit.

This is exactly the opposite of what many people believe. They believe that freedom and peace come from "doing their own thing." Before I was saved, one of my favorite songs was "I'll Do It My Way." How wrong I was! No wonder I got into so much trouble!

In the spiritual realm, success is *not* based upon "doing it our way" with our human intelligence, talents and ability. Instead, we have to *"crucify"* ourselves and adhere completely to the Lord's wishes—relying totally on Him and trusting completely in Him. "I have been *crucified* with Christ—

[in Him] I have shared His crucifixion; *it is no longer I who live, but Christ, the Messiah, lives in me;* and the life I now live in the body I *live by faith*—by adherence to and reliance on and [complete] trust—in the Son of God, Who loved me and gave Himself up for me" (Galatians 2:20, *The Amplified Bible*).

When we control our lives, we are in prison. When the Holy Spirit controls our lives, we are free! We are like eagles who are able to get into the wind currents and glide, soaring high above the earth, letting the power in the wind carry them. This is how our lives will be if we'll surrender each day to the Holy Spirit, trusting totally in His power to carry us high above the problems that seem so difficult with our limited human abilities.

In the spiritual realm, great things are accomplished *through* us, *not by us.* "...*Not* by might, *nor* by power, *but by my spirit*, saith the Lord of hosts" (Zechariah 4:6). Our lives will be transformed when they are yielded to the Holy Spirit. "And the Spirit of the Lord will come upon thee and thou...shalt be *turned into another man*" (I Samuel 10:6). When He really is in charge of our lives, His peace is our peace, His wisdom is our wisdom and His strength is our strength.

The more we yield to Him and allow Him to work in our lives, the more we will become like Him. "...as the Spirit of the Lord works within us, we become *more and more* like Him" (II Corinthians 3:18, *The Living Bible*). Confusion in our lives comes to the degree that we operate apart from the Holy Spirit. Peace comes to the degree that we are one with the Great One who lives inside of us.

Day after day He will give us fresh new insight. Often, He will show us tremendous new meaning in verses of Scripture that we have read many times

96

before. Also, He will cause us to want to obey God's Word. "...I will put my Spirit within you and cause you to *walk in* My statutes, and you shall *heed* My ordinances, and *do* them" (Ezekiel 36:27, *The Amplified Bible*).

Other living creatures throughout the universe, lacking our intelligence, have to obey God's plan for their lives. Squirrels store nuts, birds build nests and bees produce honey. All around us we see God's creatures doing what He tells them to do, the way that He tells them to do it. We need to learn their secret. We need to quiet down our souls (our intellects, emotions and willpower) and allow the Holy Spirit to take over our lives and guide us.

"We'll find the road to deep inner peace when we find God's will and follow it..."

Chapter 13

Hindrances To Peace

Everyone is looking for deep inner peace, but many of us never find it because we're looking in the wrong direction. *We can only find deep inner peace to the degree that we are able to find God's will for our lives and then yield to His will.*

God's Word tells us to glorify Him in body and in spirit. "For ye are bought with a price: therefore glorify God in your body, and in your spirit, which are God's" (1 Corinthians 6:20). Our bodies are not ours—they are God's. Our spirits are not ours—but God's.

Jesus is our example. He told the Jewish leaders that His spiritual food came from doing God's will, "Jesus said to them, My food (nourishment) is to *do the will* (pleasure) of Him Who sent Me and to *accomplish* and completely *finish* His work" (John 4:34, *The Amplified Bible*). Jesus had no interest in His personal desires and constantly sought His Father' will, "...I do *not* seek or consult My own will—I have *no* desire to do what is pleasing to Myself, My own aim, My own purpose—but *only* the will and pleasure of the Father who sent Me" (John 5:30, *The Amplified Bible*).

We find the road to deep inner peace when we find God's will for our lives and follow it. This is a narrow road—it has a narrow gate; it's difficult to find and it's difficult to stay on it. The broad road is the road of self-will, "I'll do what I want to do." This road has a wide gate; it's easy to find and it's easy to stay on.

We will find God's peace if we get on The Royal Highway—the narrow road that His Word describes, "Enter through the *narrow* gate, for *wide* is the gate and spacious and broad is the way that leads away to *destruction,* and *many* are those who are entering it. But the gate is narrow—contracted by pressure—and the way is straitened and compressed that leads away to life, and *few* are they who find it" (Matthew 7:13-14, *The Amplified Bible).*

God's Word gives us specific directions showing us how to get on this road and stay there. In addition, our Father has given us the Holy Spirit to guide us so that we can stay on this road. Will we study God's "map", His Word? Will we follow His directions? Will we allow His guide—the Holy Spirit—to keep us on it? We must because God's road is narrow; it's easy to get off the road and not even know it.

Satan's road is wide and his deceptions are very subtle. One of his deceptions is self-will, which is at the root of most of our problems. We lose the peace that our Lord has given us when we put self-will ahead of His will for our lives. The world is full of people trying to find peace and joy through pleasing themselves, never understanding that peace and joy come from pleasing God and denying ourselves.

If we live our lives the way that God's Word tells us to, His peace will flow through us like a river. "Oh, that you had *listened* to my laws! *Then you would have had peace flowing like a gentle river...*"

(Isaiah 48:18, *The Living Bible*). He will even cause our enemies to make peace with us, "When a man's ways please the Lord, *he maketh even his enemies to be at peace with him*" (Proverbs 16:7).

Through obedience we receive peace and every other blessing from God. If we don't follow the instructions that His Word gives us, it's like looking at ourselves in the mirror. We see ourselves for a short time, but the image disappears when we walk away from the mirror:

"...It is a message to *obey*, not just to listen to. So *don't* fool yourselves. For if a person just listens and doesn't obey, he is like a man looking at his face in a mirror. As soon as he walks away, he can't see himself anymore or remember what he looks like. But if anyone *keeps looking steadily* into God's law for free men he will not only remember it but he will *do* what it says, and God will greatly *bless* him in everything he does" (James 1:22-25, *The Living Bible*).

We can't deviate from God's will for our lives and still expect to receive His peace. Adam and Eve lost their peace, their oneness with God. Ever since then, all of us have inherited from them the tendency to do things our way instead of the Lord's way, "For *all* seek their *own*, not the things which are Jesus Christ's" (Philippians 2:21).

There are two contrary forces within every Christian, our old carnal nature and our new reborn spiritual nature. In each of our lives, there is a constant struggle between them. "...These two forces within us are *constantly fighting* each other to win control over us and our wishes are *never free* from their pressures" (Galatians 5:17, *The Living Bible*).

All of us constantly make the choice between the ugliness of our will and the beauty of God's will.

101

This battle goes on every day in different areas of our lives. The lower nature doesn't give up easily. It persists in fighting constantly for its selfish desires. It isn't easy to overcome it through sheer will-power. This is proven each year by the millions of people who emphatically make New Year's resolutions on January first, only to break them before the month comes to a close.

The life of Adam lives in us as our old nature. The life of Christ lives in us as our new nature. They constantly do battle against each other. Who wins the battle? *Whichever nature is fed the most!* *If we don't nourish our new nature with God's Word, it will lose the war because our old nature is fed automatically.* There are no study courses on how to worry, how to be afraid, how to be selfish, how to be lazy, how to be jealous, etc. These things come to us naturally.

We're not going to experience God's peace if our carnal, sinful nature controls our lives. Control must be shifted to our new nature. This can only be done by "reprogramming" our "computers" through a constant infusion of God's Word. We need to feed our hungry spirits constantly with the food of God's Word. The more we grow in the Lord, the more we will be able to overcome our old, carnal, selfish, prideful, lustful, fearful, evil nature that constantly tries to dominate our lives.

Many Christians who go to church each week and say their prayers each day *are still carnal Christians.* Many of us do not feed enough of God's Word into our spirits each day to overcome the power of our old nature in certain areas of our lives. Carnal people, including many Christians, insist on their own way because their unrenewed minds are hostile to God and cannot submit to God's laws. "... the mind of the flesh—with its carnal thoughts and purposes—is *hostile* to God; for it *does not submit itself* to God's Law, indeed it *cannot"* (Romans 8:7, *The Amplified Bible).*

We are spiritually immature when our lives are controlled by our own desires, "...you are still only baby Christians, controlled by your own desires, not God's..." (1 Corinthians 3:3, *The Living Bible).* Immature Christians are motivated by pride. Pride says, "I want my own way." Pride and peace don't go together. They are at opposite ends of the spiritual spectrum. The more we have of one, the less we can have of the other.

It is very easy to get caught up with our own wishes and desires, to focus on what *we* want in life. God gives us the right to do this. He gave us complete freedom of choice; however, we'll never find His peace by chasing after our own desires. A prideful attitude always causes problems.

Pride caused the mighty archangel Lucifer to be changed into the devil, Satan. Our Father detests pride—" Every one that is proud in heart is an *abomination* to the Lord..." (Proverbs 16:5). Pride destroys us and causes us to fall, "Pride goeth before *destruction,* and an haughty spirit before *a fall"* (Proverbs 16:18). Pride is destructive. Humility is constructive and leads us to peace. "...*all* who *humble* themselves before the Lord...shall have *wonderful peace"* (Psalm 37:11, *The Living Bible).*

Peace comes from being one with the Lord and this is possible only for Christians with humble, repentant hearts. "The high and lofty one who inhabits eternity, the Holy One, says this: I live in that high and holy place where those with contrite, humble spirits dwell; *and I refresh the humble* and give new courage to those with repentant hearts" (Isaiah 57:15, *The Living Bible).*

We are able to live in the same, high spiritual

103

place where our Lord lives, as long as we remain humble and contrite. If we continue in this attitude, He will refresh us, give us courage and look on us with compassion. "...I will look with pity on the man who has a humble and contrite heart..." (Isaiah 66:2, *The Living Bible*).

Many Christians who have accepted Jesus as their Saviour have *not* made Him their Master. Jesus wants to be our Master. He wants to be our Lord. He wants to be in charge of *every* aspect of our lives, *every* day of our lives. His peace is available to us if we truly do put *Him* in *first* place, *others* in *second* place and *ourselves* in *last* place.

This is God's perfect order. This is how Jesus lived during His earthly ministry. Everything that He did centered around His Father and other people. He always put Himself in last place. He wants us to do the same. *This* is the only way that His deep inner peace can be manifested in our lives.

Many of us love our husbands, wives, children or parents more than we love Jesus. This may seem right, but it isn't. "If you love your father and mother *more* than you love Me, you are *not* worthy of being Mine; or if you love your son or daughter *more* than me, you are *not* worthy of being Mine" (Matthew 10:37, *The Living Bible*).

Of course the Lord wants us to love our families unselfishly. However, the way that He wants us to do this is to surrender our entire lives to Him and to love Him with all our hearts. When we put Him first, *then* we will be able to love our families and our friends even more. Anything that comes ahead of Jesus Christ in our lives blocks us from the peace that will be ours *only* if we put Jesus first and keep Him first.

Chapter 14

The Lord Must Come First

The primary goal of every Christian should be to keep Jesus first in every area of our lives. He certainly has earned the right to be number one, for He willingly gave up the splendor of heaven and came to earth to suffer and to die a horrible death so that our sins could be forgiven. How can we possibly fail to put Him first in every area our lives??

However, this is exactly what many Christians do. Many of us go to church almost every Sunday morning, spend a few minutes in prayer each day, study the Bible a bit and engage in a few church activities. This is "it" as far as our spiritual lives are concerned.

Is *this* putting Jesus first? No, it isn't. Our Lord is looking for much more than a few hours each week. He is looking for a commitment of seven days a week, twenty-four hours each day. Many of us who have accepted Jesus as our Saviour are carnal Christians. Our lives really aren't centered around Jesus.

Too many Christians still live the way the world lives. Aside from a few hours each week, many of our lives really aren't much different from those of our friends who haven't accepted Jesus as their

Saviour. We'll never find God's peace this way. If our lives are centered predominantly on the world, our peace will tend to be fragile and elusive—largely dependent upon worldly circumstances.

How can we expect our Lord's peace and other blessings to be manifested in our lives if we spend 95% to 99% of our waking hours engaged in worldly activities and only 1% to 5% of our time, or less, in spiritual growth, worship and fellowship???

Christians shouldn't follow the world's way. We are different. God's Word says that we are unique, "peculiar" people who should contantly praise the Lord and thank Him for bringing us out of Satan's darkness into His marvelous light. "...ye are a chosen generation, a royal priesthood, an holy nation, *a peculiar people;* that ye should shew forth the praises of him who hath called you *out of darkness into his marvellous light:* which in time past were not a people, but are now the people of God: which had not obtained mercy, but now have obtained mercy" (1 Peter 2:9-10).

We're special. We are part of the royal family of God and we should act accordingly! Nothing should take priority over Jesus. We should "sell out" completely to Him. We need to go "all the way" with Him. We shouldn't be reserved about our faith, especially with unbelievers. We ought to let everyone—family, friends, other believers and unbelievers, see our total commitment to Jesus Christ.

We don't have to be offensive or pushy. It can be done in good taste with respect for the rights of others. However, we should never imply one bit less than total, absolute commitment. If people think that we're fanatics or "Jesus freaks", that's their problem, not ours.

Christians who have one foot in the church and one foot in the world experience many ups and downs. Peace doesn't come from possessions or circumstances. Peace comes from a person—Jesus Christ. When He is totally in control, life runs smoothly no matter what is going on around us. His wisdom is our wisdom. His strength is our strength. His peace is our peace. He can handle anything, but we must put Him first.

This right relationship with the Lord will cause His peace, quietness and trust to be manifested in our lives. "And the effect of righteousness shall be *peace* [internal and external], and the result of righteousness, *quietness and confident trust for ever*" (Isaiah 32:17, *The Amplified Bible*).

This is so clear! Our first goal should be to seek right standing with our Lord. We gain this right standing by putting Him first and keeping Him first in every area of our lives. *Then* we receive the manifestation of His peace.

Our Lord wants all of us! He doesn't want only part of us. He doesn't want a little bit here and a little bit there. He doesn't want what *we* find convenient. He wants our lives to be completely dedicated to and centered around Him.

The Holy Spirit should light up our lives. We should be on fire, fervently dedicated to serving Him, "...be *aglow* and *burning* with the Spirit, serving the Lord" (Romans 12:11, *The Amplified Bible*).

This isn't optional. It's a *commandment* from our Father! Jesus said, "...You shall love the Lord your God with *all* your heart, and with *all* your soul, and with *all* your mind (intellect). This is the *great* (most important, principal) and *first command-ment*" (Matthew 22:37-38, *The Amplified Bible*).

How can we love someone with all our heart, all our soul and all our mind and not have that someone come first? We can't! We must realize that this is our Lord's commandment to us—the first, the greatest and the most important commandment. *Nothing* is more important.

Our Lord doesn't want us to be "lukewarm." He wants to be so far out in front in our priorities that whatever is in second place (family, career, etc.) isn't even close! Our lives will never come into spiritual balance unless He is in absolute first place—way out in front—far, far ahead of everything else.

To experience the fullness of the Holy Spirit, we must focus first on Jesus. "Now I have *given up everything else*—I have found it to be the *only way* to *really know Christ and to experience the mighty power* that brought Him back to life again..." (Philippians 3:10, *The Living Bible*).

Jesus is the Gem of all gems. Nothing that we'll ever possess can approach the value of His kingdom. When we realize this, we'll gladly give up everything for Him; "...the kingdom of heaven is like a man who is a dealer in search of fine and precious pearls, who, on finding a single pearl of great price, went and *sold all he had* and bought it" (Matthew 13:45-46, *The Amplified Bible*).

If we continually seek the Lord with great intensity, we will find Him, "...*thou shalt find him*, if thou seek him with *all* thy heart and with *all* thy soul" (Deuteronomy 4:29). If we "delight" in Him, all of our special desires will be received. "*Delight yourself* also in the Lord, and He *will* give you the desires and secret petitions of your heart" (Psalm 37:4, *The Amplified Bible*).

Many people think that a life completely centered around the Lord is dry and uninteresting. Just the opposite is true! As we draw closer to our Lord by always keeping Him first, He will open new horizons to us. Spiritual concepts that used to be non-existent will be revealed to us. This is very exciting!

People who think that a Christ-centered life is uninteresting just don't understand. They are spiritually blind. They can't make accurate judgments if they haven't tried it. We need to put Jesus first and keep Him first all day long every day of our lives.

If we center our lives on Jesus, situations that used to perplex and frustrate us will be handled calmly and efficiently. Tension will disappear and His great peace will control our lives. Our Father wants us to surrender completely to His way of doing things, *"My son, give me your heart, and let your eyes observe and delight in my ways"* (Proverbs 23:26, *The Amplified Bible).*

How could our loving Father want anything but the best for our lives? He has a plan for each of us. It is implanted deep inside us. As we turn more and more to Him, always keeping Him first and seeking His will, He'll unfold this plan a little at a time. We'll know that we're on the right track.

A life based on human schemes and schedules will fall apart eventually. The life that seeks God's will ahead of everything else is the one that will stand up over the long haul. Our way is the wrong way. God's way is the right way.

In the spiritual realm, all success and glory is received from staying in the Lord's will. We miss God's peace when we get off track, but we gain it by getting back on the right road (His road). We live a life of continual peace by staying in His will at all times.

The highest state we can aspire to is to live constantly in God's will. The peace that all of us crave is found in the last place we might expect—in total surrender of every human desire and total submission to our Father's will for our lives.

"The Lord's deep inner peace is only available to the degree that we empty out ourselves each day of "self" and this world—and it's constant demands."

Chapter 15

Solitude—
The Key To Deep Inner Peace

So far in this book, we have discussed the peace that Jesus Christ left us, quietness and confidence in the midst of trials and tribulations, the perfect peace of God, the peace of God that passess all understanding, entering into God's rest and the great peace that is available through the Holy Spirit.

Now that we have discussed *what* is available to every Christian, we are ready to discuss very specifically *how* to manifest this peace in our lives. First, let's look at a condition that robs many people of peace—the condition of loneliness. Millions of people are extremely lonely. These people obviously do not enjoy deep inner peace. Loneliness and deep inner peace don't go together. In fact, loneliness is, in many respects, the opposite of deep inner peace.

I believe that all non-Christians are lonely. It might not seem that way for many years. This loneliness often takes a long time to manifest itself fully, but it is there. Unfortunately, many Christians are just as lonely because they live very much the way that the world lives instead of following the specific instructions that our Father has given us in His Word.

In the world, lonely people are often advised to seek new friends and to engage in more activities. This may help awhile, but no permanent relief can come from external sources. Some of the loneliest people are constantly socializing and traveling. Loneliness cannot be solved by temporary distractions. It is always waiting in the wings and when the distractions are gone, loneliness returns.

Many people are afraid to be alone. They don't have the faintest idea of what they'd do if they had to spend an hour alone—completely free of the external stimulation gained from people, telephones, radio, television, reading material, games, etc. It's not natural for people of our western culture to be quiet and still. We're always going places and doing things—much more so than people in eastern countries. Our phones ring constantly. We rush from one activity to another. Our lives are a maze of involvement.

Loneliness causes us to seek friends, join organizations and, in many cases, to get married. We're constantly going to meetings, sporting events, restaurants and movies. If there is no place to go and nothing to do, we turn on radios, watch television, talk on the phone or read books, magazines or newspapers—anything to escape being alone with our thoughts.

In recent years, more people have turned to television than any other source to fill the void of loneliness. A whole generation has grown up under the influence of television. Many readers will think that the following comments are very harsh and opinionated on the subject of television, but I sincerely believe that television is one of the greatest obstacles to finding deep inner peace. *How* can any generation develop deep inner peace with the foundation of sex, violence, and general shallowness of television programming that the majority of our people watch every day??

I recently read an article which said that television sets are turned on an average of seven hours each day in the average American household, an increase of 27% in the past ten years. The article said that women 55 years old and older watched television an average of forty-one hours a week. Television fills a vacuum in tens of millions of lives. It is the easy way out—always available with a flick of the switch.

In our parents' and grandparents' time, the home was a quiet place to rest and reflect and share time together at the end of the day. Today, virtually every home has been transformed into a small movie theatre where millions of families go to the movies each day in their own living rooms.

In fact, many families believe that they need two or more television sets so that no one will miss the programs that they want to watch. Housewives watch soap operas during the day. In the evening, virtually non-stop athletic events are available. Millions of people sit down each evening to a continuous barrage of noise, sex and violence. Then, to top it all off, many of us watch the late evening news which is filled with rape, murder, crime and often depressing news of economic conditions. After all of this, we go to bed and we wonder why we toss and turn all night and why our daily lives are so devoid of deep inner peace.

Television isn't all bad. Some programs are worthwhile. However, many television programs fill our lives with tension. Instead of relieving pressure, many of us sit with our eyes glued to see who gets murdered, who wins the girl, who escapes from the crash and who wins the ball game.

Television doesn't give us any peace. All that it

does is to fill the vacuum in our lives with fleeting enjoyment. It's virtually impossible to enjoy God's deep inner peace in an environment that is centered around several hours of subtle brainwashing from our television sets. The content of most television programming (Christian television excepted) is far from the teaching of God's Word.

Our Father wants us to *relax* in the evenings and on weekends. He created these breaks from our work so that we could spend time with Him and with our families. Television weakens many people because it is so readily accessible and because of all of the tension and sin that can be poured into our minds and hearts. The more we watch the violence and sex, the more it seems to be normal.

What kind of spiritual strength are ardent television-watchers building up for use in dealing with the crises that all of us will have to face sooner or later? We have much more leisure time than our parents, grandparents and great-grandparents had. What we do with it is the prime determining factor as to how much of God's deep inner peace we will experience.

Am I trying to say that Christians shouldn't spend some of their leisure time doing things that they enjoy doing? No, I'm not! We can enjoy hobbies. We can watch television as long as we are selective about what we watch and how long we watch it. However, all of our leisure activities should take place *in addition to* and *not instead of* our daily quiet time with the Lord.

One word is *the key* to finding deep inner peace and that word is **solitude**—an ample amount of quiet time spent alone with the Lord each day. Solitude opens the door to the Lord. We'll never find Him unless we get off by ourselves each day and seek Him with quiet time in prayer, worship, study and meditation.

It is very important for us to empty our minds and hearts of worldly activities and pre-occupation with ourselves. The Lord's deep inner peace is only available to the degree that we empty out ourselves each day of "self" and of the world and its constant demands. If we'll develop the habit of setting aside definite time with the Lord, He will work wonders in our lives, "Sanctify yourselves [that is, *separate yourselves* for special holy purpose], for tomorrow the Lord *will do wonders* among you" (Joshua 3:5, *The Amplified Bible*).

We'll never experience God's deep inner peace if our lives are always centered around seeing people, going places and doing things. We need balance. We need to offset the constant activities of the world by spending quiet time with the Lord. It's good to be busy, but it's bad to always be "on the go."

God's Word tells us that there is a time for everything, "To everything there is a season, and a time to every purpose under the heaven..." (Ecclesiastes 3:1). There is a time to work, a time to play and a time to be with our families and, *above all*, a time to be with the Lord. Just the thought of spending a considerable amount of time alone each day is too much for many people! Solitude is a prison for people who don't like their innermost thoughts and don't have any idea how to communicate with the Lord.

However, we need to realize that *aloneness* and *loneliness* are not the same. There is a big difference between the two. *Loneliness is the pain of being alone and solitude is the glory of being alone.* Loneliness and solitude are opposite sides of the same coin. Loneliness is negative. Solitude is positive. Loneliness is bad. Solitude is good. Loneliness tears down. Periods of solitude with God's Word build up. Loneliness believes that no one else cares. Solitude draws us closer to the One who cares most. In solitude we are the least alone.

We experience loneliness to the degree that we are separated from God. Sin separates us from God. Preoccupation with "self" separates us from God. Loneliness will disappear if we truly do put God first, study His Word, constantly meditating in it and living our lives according to its directions.

The atheist is always alone. Christians are never alone. Jesus is always there waiting to offer companionship, "...I have been standing at the door and I am *constantly* knocking. If anyone hears Me calling him and opens the door, *I will come in and fellowship with him and he with Me*" (Revelation 3:20, *The Living Bible*).

Our Lord is closer to us than our hands and our feet. He lives in our hearts. He is with us every minute of every hour of every day, *"I am with you always,* even to the end of the world" (Matthew 28:20, *The Living Bible*). No matter what happens, He will never abandon us, *"I will never leave thee, nor forsake thee"* (Hebrews 13:5). The Lord is our closest friend, much closer than any human friend or family member, "...there *is* a friend that sticketh *closer than a brother."* (Proverbs 18:24).

Feelings of loneliness are a clear indication that we are not turning often enough to the magnificent Presence who lives inside us. He *will* always reach out to us *if* we will reach out to Him, "...when you draw close to God, God *will* draw close to you" (James 4:8, *The Living Bible*).

We are one with the God who created us. We are one with Jesus Christ who died for us at Calvary. We are one with the same Holy Spirit who raised

Jesus from the dead. If we really know Who lives inside us, we cannot be lonely!

Jesus is our example. During His earthly ministry, He often went up into the mountains alone. "...he departed again into a mountain *himself alone*" (John 6:15). We need to get away from the crowds. We need to do what Jesus did, "And seeing the multitudes, he went up into a mountain..." (Matthew 5:1). Jesus was never lonely, "...*I am not alone, because the Father is with me*" (John 16:32).

No one has ever been any busier or more productive than Jesus was during His three-year earthly ministry. Yet, He still managed to spend long periods of time alone with His Father. He knew that these quiet times were necessary to prepare Him for constant ministering to large crowds of people. The continued fellowship with His Father gave Him the strength and power He needed. If Jesus needed this quiet time on a regular continuing basis, then we need it too! We will receive His strength, wisdom and abilities to the degree that we continually get away from the world to fellowship with Him.

A common characteristic of the truly great men and women of history is that they spent a considerable amount of time alone. This is particularly true of Christian leaders. A careful examination of the life of every Christian leader whose ministry has stood the test of time will prove this. No matter how busy they are, this precious quiet time is not overlooked. It is the basis of their success and they know it.

The world considers it normal to set aside time for physical fitness programs each day and to stick to them. However, they think it's strange if we schedule time for "spiritual exercise" each day,

"...Spend your time and energy in the exercise of keeping spiritually fit. Bodily exercise is all right, but spiritual exercise is *much more important*... (1 Timothy 4:7-8, *The Living Bible*).

We realize that our bodies need daily cleansing, food and rest. *We also need to realize that our souls require daily cleansing, food and rest.* We need to get alone with the Lord each day to take our "daily spiritual bath"—to relax and cleanse ourselves spiritually. God's Word will cleanse us and give us rest.

Jesus told His disciples, "...Come ye yourselves apart into a desert place and rest a while..." (Mark 6:31). I have often heard our pastor, Bob Ford, say, "Come apart, before you come apart." We won't manifest deep inner peace in times of stress and turmoil unless this peace has been built on a solid foundation of many hours alone with the Lord.

The world eagerly awaits a few weeks of vacation time each year. Once we learn how to break through into the spiritual realm, our Lord will give us daily vacation time that is far superior to anything the world has to offer. The greatest vacation land in existence can be found deep down inside ourselves. Our Lord wants us to spend quiet time with Him each day so that he can bring us to serenity and restore our souls. "...He leadeth me beside the *still waters*. He *restoreth my soul*..." (Psalm 23:2-3).

Loneliness actually has nothing to do with how many people are around us. It has everything to do with our daily relationship with our Lord who lives inside us. The more we learn to turn to Him each day, the less lonely we will be. Finally, all loneliness will disappear and the most glorious part of each day will be the quiet time we spend with our Divine Companion.

Spiritual maturity is measured by our degree of spiritual comfort when we are alone. Solitude is a prison for the person who is spiritually dead but it is a paradise to the person who is spiritually alive and growing. When we set time aside to be with the Lord, we're not running away from the problems that we face in the world. Instead, we're moving towards the Lord so that we will be better equipped to handle them. We must get this continual quiet time with the Lord. *This is the foundation for deep inner peace!*

"There is a whole new world out there, a separate, eternal, spiritual realm that completely dominates and controls this temporary worldly realm that we live in..."

Chapter 16

Drawing Closer To The Lord

When Jesus was here on earth, everyone wanted to be with Him. Great crowds surrounded Him. Today, *every* Christian has an opportunity to spend this time with Jesus because He lives inside of us. He is with us all day long, every day of our lives, waiting to spend time fellowshipping with us. The more time we spend fellowshipping with Him, the closer we'll draw to Him.

It is very important to realize what an invaluable right it is to have the opportunity to constantly draw closer to our Lord, "...I count everything as loss compared to the possession of the *priceless privilege*—the overwhelming preciousness, the surpassing worth and supreme advantage—of *knowing* Christ Jesus my Lord, and of *progressively becoming more deeply and intimately acquainted with Him*, of perceiving and recognizing and understanding Him *more fully and clearly*. For His sake I have lost everything and consider it all to be mere rubbish (refuse, dregs), in order that I may win (gain) Christ, The Anointed One..." (Philippians 3:8, *The Amplified Bible*).

The Apostle Paul is telling us here that everything else is worthless—lost time and rubbish—compared to time spent drawing closer to our Lord.

He is telling us that we have a priceless privilege and a supreme advantage in being able to draw closer to our Lord, to get to know Him better and better and to understand more of what He is trying to teach us.

If I ask any reader of this book, "Do you love Jesus?", most of you would say, "Of course I do!" *If we really love someone, don't we want to spend a lot of time with them?? Don't we want to draw closer and closer to them??* We may say that we love the Lord, but many of us will have to admit that we don't spend a lot of time each day drawing closer to Him.

Many of us are throwing away a precious, priceless privilege. How can we say that we love the Lord if we spend only a little time with Him each day? *We wouldn't dream of neglecting our worldly friends the way that many of us neglect Jesus!*

There is a whole new world out there, a separate, eternal, spiritual realm that completely dominates and controls this temporary worldly realm that we live in. We will learn more and more about this separate dimension by constantly getting to know our Lord better. As Christians, it is very important for us to find this spiritual realm and enter into it. Jesus said that we are *not* of this world. "They are *not* of the world (worldly, belonging to the world), [just] as I am *not* of the world" (John 17:16, *The Amplified Bible*).

Each day, we need to *get away from* the worldly realm of people, places, things and events. We need to enter into another dimension—a world where there is no fear, no worry and no hurry—a place where there is total and complete peace at all times.

As we spend time with the Lord each day, studying, meditating, worshipping, praying, rejoicing and fellowshipping with Him, His goodness and tranquility will be multiplied in our lives, *"Grace and peace be multiplied unto you through the knowledge of God, and of Jesus our Lord..."* (2 Peter 1:2). God's grace is His kindness, favors that he gives us even though we haven't earned them. We can *multiply* His grace and peace by constantly drawing closer and closer to Him. However, this isn't easy. Many Christians try, *but few persevere.*

In the spiritual realm, our hearts are the soil and God's Word is the seed. The renewed mind is like tilled soil. The unrenewed mind is like hard clay. We need to till the soil and plant God's seed continually. Satan will do his best to steal this seed from our hearts before it has a chance to take root and start to produce a harvest of spiritual understanding and comprehension, "While any one is hearing the Word of the kingdom and does not grasp and comprehend it, *the evil one comes and snatches away what is sown in his heart..."* (Matthew 13:19, *The Amplified Bible*).

If we're persistent, this seed will grow and great spiritual fruit will be produced in our lives as this seed reproduces itself many times over, "As for what was sown on *good soil*, this is *he who hears the Word and grasps and comprehends it; he indeed bears fruit,* and yields in one case, a hundred times as much as was sown, and in another sixty times as much, and in another thirty" (Matthew 13:23, *The Amplified Bible*).

We should persist in setting aside spiritual time each day, whether or not we're seeing immediate results. A lot of growth can take place deep down inside of us when we're not aware of it. It takes time for roots to form, for the sprout to push its way through the crust of the soil and for a harvest to be reaped.

We must be patient and persistent. If we persist with quiet, calm diligence and trust, sooner or later, we will experience a spiritual breakthrough. After awhile, it will happen again. Then it will happen again...and again...and again.

Slowly but surely we'll climb more and more out of the realm of the senses and into the spiritual realm. It's like climbing a mountain. We can see very little when we're down in the valley, but the higher we climb the broader our vision becomes and the more we comprehend. Too many of us quit before we climb very far. As a result, we never get off the ground spiritually.

If we persist faithfully, our daily quiet time with the Lord soon will change from a duty to a blessing. During those first few months when many of us grind it out with no apparent results, it is a duty. We can't break the habits of a lifetime in a few weeks. Once we break through the initial barriers, our quiet time with the Lord each day will become a tremendous blessing, the absolute center of our lives!

When we spend quiet time with the Lord each day, we're actually setting up a transmitting station that is able to direct waves of communication between the spiritual realm and the natural realm. The more we do this, the less "static" there will be and the better our reception will become.

As we spend more and more quiet time with the Lord, He'll give us more and more glimpses into The Great Unseen. Each day will be a new adventure. God's ways are too vast for us to grasp all at once. As we keep turning to Him, He keeps pulling the veil back a little more, revealing a little at a time.

This is God's kingdom—a kingdom that can be entered only if we consistently turn away from preoccupation with the world and turn towards preoccupation with the Lord. God's Kingdom is inside of us. We enter into this kingdom to the degree that we comprehend God's laws which already have been placed within us. "...I *will* imprint My laws upon their *minds* even upon their innermost thoughts and understanding, *and engrave them upon their hearts...*" (Hebrews 8:10, *The Amplified Bible).*

When we are reborn spiritually, God puts all of His great spiritual truth deep inside of us. We already have inside of ourselves everything that we'll ever need. We must enter into the spiritual realm each day in order to *bring out* more of the great truth that has already been placed inside of us.

As we do this, we'll learn to follow His leading more and more. We'll do things that don't seem important to us because He tells us they are important. Conversely, we'll ignore worldly circumstances that seem to cry out for attention because our increased spiritual perception will show us that they aren't urgent and, in fact, are insignificant.

It's a whole new world—a world that is awesome in its beauty and simplicity. As we turn more and more to the Lord, life will become much less complex and confusing. We have been given very clear, definite laws to follow.

Our Father will bless us mightily if we seek Him with all our hearts and do what His Word tells us to do. "Blessed, happy, fortunate [to be envied] are they who *keep His testimonies, and who seek, inquire for and of Him and crave Him with the whole heart"* (Psalm 119:2, *The Amplified Bible).* The Lord will bless us wonderfully if we'll seek Him with all our hearts and live our lives the way that His Word tells us to live them.

"Continual meditation on God's Word keeps us on His "wave length" and in harmony with Him."

Chapter 17

The Benefits Of God's Word In Our Hearts

There is only one way to bridge the gap between the seen and the unseen, the natural realm and the spiritual realm. The bridge between these two realms is the Word of God. We are so little. God is so big. He has given us a Book of Instructions that shows us how to get out of our little world and into His big world. He has given us the Holy Spirit to guide us in understanding His Book. "...when he, the Spirit of truth, is come, *he will guide you into all truth..."* (John 16:13).

We have been given everything we need. *Will we use it?* Will we listen with great anticipation to what our Father tells us in His Word? If we will, we'll hear the words of peace that we long to hear, "I will listen [with expectancy] to what God the Lord will say, for *He will speak peace* to His people..." (Psalm 85:8, *The Amplified Bible*).

Mistakes are inevitable when we do things our way. It is imperative for us to learn God's way. His Word tells us exactly how to enjoy His great peace, *"Great peace have they who love Your law; nothing shall offend them or make them stumble"* (Psalm 119:165, *The Amplified Bible*).

If we *really do* love God's Word, we will enjoy great peace. Because we love it, we'll study and meditate in it continually. As a result, nothing will be able to make us stumble. No matter how difficult our problems might be, nothing will be able to rob us of His great peace.

This great peace comes from a heart that is filled with the Word of God. It should always be there, just below the surface, ready to be called upon at an instant's notice. When a seeming crisis confronts us, our "computer" (our mind) should scan our data storage bank (our heart) and immediately come up with several specific promises from our Father that will enable us to overcome the problem.

If our hearts are full of God's Word and if we do what it says, we'll live long, full, tranquil lives, "My son, *forget not* my law or teaching, but *let your heart keep my commandments;* for *length of days,* and *years of a life [worth living],* and *tranquility,* [inward and outward and *continuing* through old age till death], these shall they add to you" (Proverbs 3:1-2, *The Amplified Bible).*

We will live a glorious life if we'll just fill our hearts with the Word of God and do what it says to do. I can't emphasize too often that this must be a continual process. Yesterday's spiritual food won't do the job today. If we go two or three days without feeding God's Word into hearts, we will start to experience "spiritual malnutrition."

If we love God's Word, we'll "delight" in it. If we delight in it, we will meditate in it continually. Meditation means to fix our attention on a particular verse (or verses) of Scripture and to constantly turn this over and over in our minds, looking at it from every angle. (For a thorough explanation of meditation, see chapters 5 and 6 of my book *Trust God For Your Finances.)*

If we delight in God's Word and meditate in it

constantly, we'll establish deep spiritual roots that cannot be shaken. Then we will succeed and bear fruit in every area of our lives, "...his *delight* is in the law of the Lord; and in his law *doth he meditate day and night.* And he shall be like a tree planted by the rivers of water, that *bringeth forth his fruit* in his season; his leaf also shall *not* wither; *and whatsoever he doeth shall prosper"* (Psalm 1:2-3).

Continual meditation quiets our minds and emotions and brings them into alignment with our Father. We're in harmony with another person when we're on the same "wave length" that they're on. Continual meditation in God's Word keeps us on His "wave length" and keeps us in harmony with Him.

There's a very distinct relationship between meditation and deep inner peace. However, there are "counterfeits" for meditation in God's Word, such as yoga, transcendental meditation, etc. They have the right principle, but they're meditating on the wrong things. Our Father's deep inner peace will come to us only when we're meditating on great spiritual truth—truth that can be found only in His Word.

When we meditate, we turn to God and ask Him to reveal the great truths that we need to know. If we'll meditate calmly and quietly each day, He will reveal them, *"Call to Me and I will answer you and show you great and mighty things, fenced in and hidden, which you do not know—do not distinguish and recognize, have knowledge of and understand"* (Jeremiah 33:3, *The Amplified Bible*).

I believe that the way to receive these great truths is to study God's Word each morning and then to meditate on it continually throughout the day and night. It is much better studying God's Word early in the morning than trying to set aside time in the midst of a hectic, busy day. In these precious, quiet moments before the phones start ringing and people start talking, hurrying and worrying, we can be alone with our Lord.

Jesus often got up long before daybreak so that he could have quiet communion with His Father, "And *in the morning*, rising up a *great while before day*, he went out, and departed into a solitary place, and there prayed" (Mark 1:35). Those precious early hours were of great benefit to Jesus and they will benefit us, too. If we seek the Lord early in the morning, we will find Him, "...those who seek me *early* and *diligently* shall *find me*" (Proverbs 8:17, *The Amplified Bible*). Our Father wants us to hear Him each morning, "...He wakens me *morning* by *morning*, He wakens my ear to hear as disciples— as those who are taught" (Isaiah 50:4, *The Amplified Bible*).

When we spend quiet time with the Lord in the morning, we build a beautiful foundation for the day ahead. We line ourselves up with His will and the strength and guidance that we receive enable us to carry His calm quietness with us throughout the day.

Then, throughout the day and night, we should meditate continually on God's Word, turning it over and over in our minds and speaking it constantly with our mouths. If we follow this process each day, our hearts will be filled with more and more of God's precious Word and we'll experience more and more of His deep inner peace.

The Bible is a window that enables us to see God. The more we study and meditate in it, the more we'll be able to see and understand His great spiritual truths. These truths are multi-faceted. God's Word is like a beautiful diamond—when we hold it up to the light, its brilliance and dimensions are awesome and beautiful. Like a diamond, when we turn the Word of God to a slightly different angle, we see new, sparkling aspects that weren't visible before.

As we study and meditate continually on the Word of God, it will enter into our hearts and great spiritual truth will unfold. "The entrance and unfolding of Your words gives *light;* it gives *understanding—discernment* and *comprehension*—to the simple" (Psalm 119:130, *The Amplified Bible).* As the purity of the Lord is revealed, our hearts will rejoice. "The precepts of the Lord are right, *rejoicing the heart;* the commandment of the Lord is *pure and bright, enlightening the eyes..."* (Psalm 19:8, *The Amplified Bible).* There is nothing more thrilling than a life that is illuminated each day with the light of God's Word!

Our Father wants very much to reveal Himself to us. He will become more and more real to us as we seek Him with all our heart and hunger for His spiritual food. Then, He'll give us profound satisfaction, *"For He satisfies the longing soul, and fills the hungry soul with good"* (Psalm 107:9, *The Amplified Bible).*

If we turn continually to the Lord each day, He will satisfy our spiritual hunger and thirst, "...I am the Bread of Life. He who comes to Me *will never be hungry* and he who believes on and cleaves to and trusts in and relies on Me *will never thirst any more*—at any time" (John 6:35, *The Amplified Bible).*

Life is full and complete when we are constantly drawing closer to the Master. Each day we will look forward to quiet time with Him, eagerly awaiting the next morsels of truth. Nothing can compare with the precious times of enlightenment when our Lord reveals more of His great wisdom.

This even offsets the aging process. As we grow

older chronologically, the effect of the years will be lessened if spiritual renewal is constantly going on inside of us. Fear, discouragement, weariness and psychosomatic illnesses won't be able to get a foothold if we renew our minds each and every day. "...*we do not become discouraged—utterly spiritless, exhausted, and wearied out through fear. Though our outer man is (progressively) decaying and wasting away, yet our inner self is being (progressively) renewed day after day*" (2 Corinthians 4:16, *The Amplified Bible*).

Wisdom and understanding will give us everything that the world craves. They lead us to happiness. They are much more valuable than the riches that many people seek. Nothing can compare to a life that is filled with wisdom and understanding from God's Word. The world searches for fame, fortune and a long, pleasant, peaceful life, but better things are available to those who find wisdom and get understanding.

"*Happy* is the man that findeth *wisdom*, and the man that getteth *understanding*. For the merchandise of it is *better* than the merchandise of *silver*, and the gain thereof than fine *gold*. She is *more precious* than *rubies:* and all the things thou canst desire are *not* to be compared unto her. *Length of days* is in her right hand; and in her left hand *riches* and *honour. Her ways are ways of pleasantness, and all her paths are peace*" (Proverbs 3:13-17).

Many of us block the wisdom of God because we depend upon our own wisdom. If we humbly approach Him, admitting how little we know and how much we need to learn from Him, His pure, gentle wisdom will lead us to peace. "...the wisdom that is from above is first *pure*, then *peaceable*, *gentle...*" (James 3:17).

There is a lot of confusion in what is being taught in the world today. Different "religions" teach different concepts. Different Christian teachers teach different concepts. How can we get rid of all of this confusion and find the truth? There is only one way and that is to fill our hearts with the Word of God. *Knowledge comes in from the outside. Wisdom comes out from the inside.*

We'll never be able to weed out all of the false teaching and spiritual misconception unless our hearts are filled with the Word of God. Satan wants us to be confused, but God doesn't. He wants us to be at peace. *"...God is not the author of confusion, but of peace..."* (1 Corinthians 14:33).

If we're confused, we're not at peace. If we're confused, we're not putting our trust in the Lord. We can only overcome confusion by trusting completely in Him. "In thee, O Lord, do I put my trust: *let me never be put to confusion"* (Psalm 71:1).

There isn't going to be any confusion in heaven because Satan won't be there, but we don't have to put up with confusion here on earth, either! The truth of God's Word will drive out the lies and misconceptions that Satan tries to foist on us and will show him to be the lying, cheating, powerless bluffer that he really is.

All of us will have to deal with our share of problems. In God's eyes, *the important thing isn't what happens to us in this life, but how we react to what happens to us.* Will we react based upon our emotions? Will we react based upon fear, doubt, and unbelief? Or, will we refuse to be confused and maintain our peace because we are determined not to react to anything except the precious Word of God?

If we have spent the quiet time with the Lord that we should have, His strong, quiet peace will be in our hearts when we are hit hard by the adversities of life. With this peace, we *can* keep our equilibrium in this topsy-turvy, unbalanced world. Our daily quiet time with the Lord is *the anchor* that will hold us steady when the storms of life come at us.

Most battles are won or lost based upon the thoroughness of preparation for them before they start. If we spend adequate amounts of time alone with the Lord each day, we'll build a fire deep down inside of us that cannot be extinguished by the problems of life. No matter how severe these attacks might be, the strength and wisdom of our Lord is greater.

He knows exactly where we are, where we need to go and how to get us there. He'll guide us through the problem if we are able to relax and trust Him. When we're relaxed and trusting, this opens the door for us to receive ideas from heaven that will solve every problem here on earth. We're *not* at the mercy of life's problems. God's Word and the Holy Spirit within us are much, much greater than any problems!

Chapter 18

Calm, Patient Contentment

We have been through a lot of material on the subject of deep inner peace. If we will study and assimilate this, it will calm us down. We will become much more calm and patient. This is what our Father wants.

He doesn't want us to complain about anything. *"In everything you do, stay away from complaining..."* (Philippians 2:14, *The Living Bible*). If we complain, we show our *lack* of deep inner peace. If we are growing spiritually, we'll learn to be calm no matter what happens to us. *"...I have learned, in whatsoever state I am, therewith to be content"* (Philippians 4:11).

The Greek word that is translated "content" in this verse of Scripture means "independent of circumstances." Christians should remain calm regardless of the circumstances in our lives. We should react only to God's Word. A state of contentment doesn't come to us overnight. The Apostle Paul said that he has "learned" how to be content. Contented people are calm and unhurried.

Americans hurry more than any other people in the world. The high pressure atmosphere that we live in is conducive to hurry. The bigger the city, the more people seem to hurry. The pace is much

135

slower in other countries. It's not easy to find deep inner peace in the hectic atmosphere that prevails in the United States.

We might expect an extremely rapid pace in the business world, but it doesn't stop there. Millions of Americans are on a constant treadmill. This is particularly evident in families with young children. They're always on the go—baseball, football, basketball, hockey, soccer, scouts, school activities, etc. There *isn't* anything wrong with these activities *if* God is first in the family. However, in many cases all of these activities block God from more than a few moments of prayer each day and a short time in church on Sunday morning.

There is *no* hurrying and rushing in the spiritual realm. Hurry is man-made. God's Word says that those who trust in Him will not rush or hurry, "...he that believeth *shall not make haste*" (Isaiah 28:16). In the natural realm, great significance is given to speed and strength. The *opposite* is true in the spiritual realm, "...*the race is not to the swift, nor the battle to the strong...*" (Ecclesiastes 9:11).

In the spiritual realm, victory comes to those who slow down and trust the Lord, trusting in *His* strength and ability instead of our strength and ability. "...flight shall be *lost* to the swift and refuge shall *fail him;* the strong shall *not* retain and confirm his strength, *neither* shall the mighty deliver himself" (Amos 2:14, *The Amplified Bible).*

Hurry takes the joy out of living and robs us of the peace the Lord has given us. Hurry rhymes with worry and it should because the two go together. *Hurry is worry in action.* Hurry is caused by tension. Tension makes simple jobs seem hard and hard jobs seem impossible. Tension causes emotional fatigue and drains our energy.

Tension wastes energy and it shortens our lives. It is a major cause of indigestion, heartburn, and ulcers. Hurry and tension have contributed significantly to the increase in nervous breakdowns, strokes, heart disease and cancer. The word, "disease" means "lack of ease". Our lack of ease (lack of peace) make us get sick. When this lack of ease is replaced by deep inner peace founded upon the Lord Jesus Christ, we are on the road to avoiding emotionally-induced illness.

There is no need to rush. We're going to live forever. Worry and hurry create spiritual static which blocks us from hearing the still, small voice of the Holy Spirit. He doesn't holler at us. He whispers. We can only hear His whisper when we are calm and quiet inside.

He speaks to us constantly, but many of us don't hear Him. If we want to hear, we must turn away from the world. If we want to communicate with Him, we need to keep our lives simple. Too many of us block His still, small voice by all of our activities.

This includes church activities. **Many of us get so caught up trying to work "for" God that we're never quiet long enough to hear what He wants us to do!** Our Father isn't as interested in how many meetings we attend as He is in having us hear Him when He speaks to us.

We must learn to relax and wait on Him. If we need an answer and the answer isn't immediately forthcoming, we shouldn't press trying to force the issue. Instead, we should say, "I don't see an answer, but the Holy Spirit does. My timing isn't important. His timing is perfect. I may think I need an answer right away, but He knows better. I'm going to remain calm. I won't try to force a solution. I'm going to wait on Him because I trust completely in Him."

When we hurry and try to make things happen, we actually are saying, "I can't wait on you, Lord. I'm going to have to take care of this myself." Too many of us go charging out ahead of the Lord. Our attitude says, "Come on, Lord. Catch up to me. We've got to get moving!" How foolish this is. This is just the opposite of what God's Word tells us to do, *"Rest in the Lord, and wait patiently for Him..."* (Psalm 37:7).

Sometimes the hardest thing is to do nothing. However, many times this is exactly what the Lord wants us to do, "...learn to *put aside your own desires* so that you will become *patient and godly, gladly letting God have His way with you"* (2 Peter 1:6, *The Living Bible).*

The world says, "He who hesitates is lost." As is often the case, this is exactly the opposite of what God's Word says! We need to hesitate in order to wait on the Lord, *"Wait on the Lord:* be of good courage, and he shall strengthen thine heart: *wait,* I say, on the Lord" (Psalm 27:14).

We need to know that if something is of the Lord, it will still be there if we hesitate long enough to seek His will. We don't have to decide immediately. The Lord has His own way of doing things and He has His own timing. We shouldn't try to second-guess Him, *"It is not for you to know the times or the seasons,* which the Father hath put in his own power" (Acts 1:7). It's easy to race on ahead. This doesn't take any skill at all. It's not easy to wait on the Lord. We need to learn to do this.

When we need to be creative under pressure, we must relax. A spontaneous, trusting attitude opens channels that a rigid, worried attitude blocks. Minds filled with tension are not creative. Creativity doesn't flow in a hurried, hectic atmosphere.

It flows out of an atmosphere of quiet, confident trust.

The world thinks that power comes from action. In the spiritual realm, power is released through human inaction. Speed is always at the expense of power. When we're still, we align ourselves with the Source of all power, *"...you shall receive power— ability, efficiency and might—when the Holy Spirit has come upon you..."* (Acts 1:8, *The Amplified Bible*).

Spiritual power comes from a calm, peaceful center. It comes out of quietness deep down inside of us. If we will withdraw each day from the noise and confusion of the world to spend time in the Master's presence, *we will build up the deep inner peace and the reservoir of spiritual power that we need.*

Conclusion

When we started this book, we started with a verse of Scripture that tells us that our Father has called His children to live in peace, "...God hath *called us to peace"* (1 Corinthians 7:15). We saw that our Father wants us to search eagerly for peace, "...*search for peace*—harmony, undisturbedness from fears, agitating passions and moral conflicts—*and seek it eagerly.*—Do not merely desire peaceful relations [with God, with your fellowmen, and with yourself], but *pursue,* go after them!" (1 Peter 3:11, *The Amplified Bible).*

We have searched for the peace that our Father has called us to. We have gone through eighteen chapters that are full of detail concerning what God's Word teaches us about peace, "...correctly analyzing and accurately dividing—rightfully handling and skillfully teaching—the Word of Truth" (2 Timothy 2:15, *The Amplified Bible).*

In these final days before Jesus comes again, the world is going to go through some turbulent times. *Now* is the time for us to learn to be more and more quiet on the inside, regardless of what is happening on the outside. When Jesus comes, He wants to find us at peace, "...*be eager* to be found by Him [at His coming] without spot or blemish, and *at peace*—in serene confidence, free from fears and agitating passions and moral conflicts" (2 Peter 3:14, *The Amplified Bible).*

What will you do with this book now that you have read it once? I pray, that instead of just putting it down, you will go back and carefully *study* it. This isn't just another book. It is filled with the power and truth of God's Word.

This is a practical, thorough book. It will simplify many areas that confuse many Christians. It is written in plain English. It isn't difficult to understand. Please go back through this book and read it carefully. Take notes. Meditate on God's great truths. Follow the recommended principles. The truths from God's Word will dramatically change the life of any reader who will study and meditate on them.

We need to learn to develop our own deep inner peace so that we will react properly in times of crisis. We also need to develop this deep inner peace so that we can help others. One of the best ways to reach out to other people is for them to see our deep inner peace when we are faced with severe problems. When everything is going wrong and we are able to relax completely and trust in the Lord, other people will want the quiet, calm peace that they see in us. Peace is contagious. When God's deep inner peace dominates our lives, we will be able to reach out to others and share these principles with them to help them develop their own deep inner peace.

Life is complicated when we do things our way, but it's simple if we follow our Father's instructions. Serenity comes from simplicity. *I pray in the Name of the Lord Jesus Christ that every person who reads this book will pay the price to study and meditate on our Father's instructions, follow these instructions, and then share what they have learned with others who so badly need this deep inner peace.*

What Did You Learn From This Book?

One way of finding out how much you have retained from this book is to take the following test. How many answers do you know now—while this book is still fresh in your mind? I suggest that you mark your calendar to take this test again on a specific date—thirty to ninety days from now, to check your retention after a period of time.

This book will only help you to the degree that it can persuade you to change your habits to line up with the instruction that our Father has given us to follow if we want to receive His peace. How many answers do you know to the following questions?

Question	Page Ref.
1. What specific instructions does the Word of God give us on how to search for peace?	8
2. What is the "seed" that must be planted in order to produce "fruit" of peace?	10
3. Where do we plant this seed?	10
4. What is the one specific thing that all Christians should be aware of in regard to seeking peace through recreation, hobbies, vacations and other worldly activities?	14

Appendix

Have You Entered
Into The Kingdom Of God?

You have just read a complete summary of God's Word pertaining to the subject of peace. These are laws that our Father has written for His children—those human beings who have entered into His kingdom. I ask each reader of this book, "Have *you* entered into the kingdom of God?"

Jesus Christ said, "...Verily, verily, I say unto thee, except a man be born again, he cannot see the kingdom of God" (John 3:3). Jesus went on to say, "...ye must be born again" (John 3:7). It is very clear that there is only one way to enter into the kingdom of God and that is to be "born again."

We don't enter into God's kingdom by church attendance, by teaching Sunday School, by baptism, by confirmation or by living a good life. Jesus Christ paid the price for every one of us to enter into God's kingdom, but this is not "automatic." Many people are so caught up with their own religious denomination or their own personal beliefs that they completely miss God's specific instructions as to how to enter into His kingdom—for the rest of our lives on earth and also for eternity in heaven.

In order to become a born-again Christian, we first of all, must admit that we are sinners (Romans 3:23, James 2:10). We must admit that there is absolutely no way that we can enter into God's kingdom based upon our own merits. Next, we have to genuinely repent of our sins (Luke 13:3, Acts 3:19).

After this admission of sin and repentance there is one additional step that must be taken in order to become a born-again Christian. "For if you *tell others* with your own mouth that Jesus Christ is your Lord, and *believe* in your own heart that God has raised Him from the dead, you *will* be saved. For it is by believing in his *heart* that a man becomes right with God; and with his *mouth* he tells others of his faith, confirming his salvation" (Romans 10:9-10, *The Living Bible*).

Many people know that Jesus Christ died for our sins. However, knowledge isn't enough. Intellectual agreement isn't enough. In order to be born again, we have to accept Jesus as our Saviour in our *hearts* and not just in our heads. We're not born again until we come to Him as admitted sinners and trust Him deep down in our hearts as the only way that we can enter into the kingdom of God. God knows exactly what we believe deep down in our hearts (I Samuel 16:7, I Chronicles 28:9 Hebrews 4:13).

We must believe in our hearts that Jesus Christ is the Son of God, that He was born of a virgin, that He died on the cross to pay for our sins, that He rose again from the dead and that He lives today. In order to be a born-again Christian, Romans 10:9-10 tells us that we must not only believe this in our hearts, but we *also* must open our *mouths* and tell others of this belief. This confirms our salvation.

When you believe this in your heart and tell others of this belief with your mouth, *then* you are a born-again Christian. All of us were born naturally on the day that our mothers gave birth to us. We must have a second birth—a spiritual birth—in order to enter into God's kingdom. "For you have a new life. It was not passed on to you from your parents, for the life they gave you will fade away. This new one will last forever, for it comes from Christ, God's ever-living Message to men" (I Peter 1:23, *The Living Bible).*

God wants us to come to Him, not as intellectuals, but as little children. God doesn't reveal Himself to us through our intellects. He reveals Himself to us through our hearts and, in order to enter into His kingdom, we must come to Him as little children. We may be adults in the natural world, but in the spiritual world we have to start all over. We have to be born again as spiritual babies. Jesus said, "...except ye be converted and become as little children, ye shall not enter into the kingdom of heaven" (Matthew 18:3).

The following prayer will cause you to become born again if you believe this in your heart and open your mouth and tell others of this belief:

"Dear Father, I come to You in the Name of Jesus Christ. I admit that I am a sinner and I know that there is no way I can enter into Your kingdom based upon the sinful life that I have led. I'm genuinely sorry for my sins and I ask for Your mercy. I believe in my heart that Jesus Christ is Your Son— that He was born of a virgin, that He died on the cross to pay for my sins, that You raised Him from the dead and that He is alive today. I trust in Him as my only way of entering into Your kingdom. I confess now to You, Father, that Jesus Christ is my Saviour and my Lord and I will tell others of this decision now and in the future. Thank You, Father. Amen."

When you believe this in your heart and confess this to others with your mouth, you have been reborn spiritually. You are brand new in the spiritual realm. "Therefore if any man be in Christ, he is a *new* creature: old things are *passed away;* behold, *all* things have become new" (II Corinthians 5:17).

Now that you have a new, recreated spirit, you are ready to study, understand and obey God's laws pertaining to peace and all of His other laws. This will transform the rest of your life on earth and you also will live forever in heaven. "For God so loved the world, that he gave his only begotten Son, that whosoever believeth in him should not perish, but have everlasting life" (John 3:16).

Other Books By Jack Hartman

God's Promise:
"All Sufficiency In All Things."

Jack Hartman

TRUST GOD FOR YOUR FINANCES

Jack Hartman is a self-employed businessman. In 1974, he was on the verge of bankruptcy and a nervous break-down. He was almost para-lyzed by worry and fear. At that time he accepted Jesus Christ as Saviour and Lord.

He immediately started to study and meditate day and night in the Holy Scriptures to learn how to solve his financial and emotional problems. After several months of study he was able to apply these Biblical principles to his problems and they worked!

His business has turned completely around, all debts have been paid off right on schedule and his business has grown steadily each year since then. In addition, he and three other businessmen started a Bible study class in his office which now has grown into a large church with average Sunday morning attendance of 1,000 people.

The growth of this business and the growth of this church have come as a result of applying Biblical principles which Jack has explained in his book *Trust God For Your Finances.*

The principles in this book are not theoretical. They have worked in Jack Hartman's life and in the lives of many people who have counseled with him. Now these principles are available in book form.

Jack carefully points out the differences between the world's system of prosperity and God's laws of prosperity. He explains that all of the warnings in the Bible against financial prosperity are warnings against following the *world's* system of prosperity.

Our Father very *definitely* wants His children to prosper as long as they follow His laws of prosperity. These laws are laid out in detail in sixteen chapters of specific instruction—every chapter filled with many verses of Scripture.

Trust God For Your Finances can be ordered for $4.95 per copy plus 10% postage and handling. The order form for this is at the end of this book.

NUGGETS OF FAITH

Jack Hartman

As soon as Mr. Hartman accepted Christ as his personal Savior, he began an intensive study of God's Word. From the very first day of this study and meditation the Lord led him to write "Spiritual Meditations" on the spiritual truths that he learned that day. He now has written over 20,000 (!) of these meditations and he continues to write them almost every day of his life.

Mr. Hartman has now written a book of his best spiritual meditations on the subject of faith. The title of this book is *Nuggets of Faith.* There are over eighty of these "nuggets" (average length—3 paragraphs) which are the result of thousands of hours of research and study.

There are no wasted words in this book. Each of these "nuggets" goes straight to the point. This book will give you maximum results in a minimum of time. It will make you think.

You can easily read this book in one day. On the other hand, each of these "nuggets" contains enough depth so that you can take one "nugget" with you in the morning and dwell on it throughout the day, turning its scriptural truth over and over in your mind as you meditate on how this scriptural truth can apply to your life.

Nuggets of Faith can be ordered for $2.50 per copy plus 10% postage and handling. The order form for this is at the end of this book.

Cassette Tapes
By Jack Hartman

Tape #   **Title**

01H **How To Study The Bible (Part I)**—21 scriptural reasons why it is so important to study the Bible.

02H **How To Study The Bible (Part II)**—a step-by-step detailed explanation of a proven effective system for studying the Bible (our most demanded tape).

03H **Enter Into God's Rest**—Don't struggle and strain with loads that are too heavy for you. Learn exactly what God's Word teaches about relaxing under pressure.

04H **Freedom From Worry**—a comprehensive scriptural explanation on how to become completely free from worry.

05H **God's Strength—Our Weakness**—God's strength is available to the degree that we can admit our human weakness and trust, instead, in His unlimited strength.

06H **How To Transform Our Lives**—a thorough, scriptural study of how we can change our lives completely through a complete spiritual renewal of our minds.

07H **The Greatest Power In The Universe (Part I)**—the greatest power in the universe is love. Part I gives a beautiful scriptural explanation of our Father's love for us.

08H **The Greatest Power In The Universe (Part II)**—a thorough scriptural explanation on our love for God, our love for each other and overcoming fear through love.

09H **How Well Do You Know Jesus Christ?**—an Easter Sunday message that received great audience response. After this message, you'll know Jesus Christ as you never knew Him before.

10H **God's Perfect Peace**—In a world of unrest, people everywhere are searching for inner peace. This is a detailed scriptural explanation of how to obtain God's perfect peace.

11H **Freedom Through Surrender**—Millions of people are trying to find freedom by "doing their own thing." God's Word tells us to do just the opposite. Freedom comes only as a result of daily surrender of our lives to Jesus Christ.

12H **Overcoming Anger**—Do you know when anger is permissible and when it is a sin? Learn step-by-step procedures from the Bible on how to overcome the sinful effects of anger.

13H **Taking Possession Of Our Souls**—God's Word teaches that patience is the key to the possession of our souls. Learn why God allows us to have severe problems, why He sometimes makes us wait for His answer and how to increase patience and endurance.

14H **Staying Young In The Lord**—Our generation tries to cover up the aging process with makeup, hair coloring, hairpieces, etc. The Bible teaches us a better way. Learn specific factual methods to offset the aging process.

15H **Two Different Worlds**—A specific explanation of how to enter into the spiritual realm in order to learn the great truths that our Father wants to reveal to us.

16H **Trust God For Your Finances**—We have have many requests for a cassette tape of Jack Hartman's book "Trust God For Your Finances." In response to this request, this tape was made and it contains a summary of the highlights of the book.

A Request To Our Readers

Has this book helped you? If so, would you be willing to tell others so that this book can help them too? Many people are naturally skeptical about the advertising claims for a book such as this. This is why we use a large number of "testimonials" from satisfied readers in our advertising for this book.

If this book has helped you, I'd appreciate it if you would write to me in care of the publisher. Please tell me in your own words how this book has helped you and why you would recommend it to others. Please give us as much information as you can.

Also, we will need your written permission to use any part or all of your comments, your name and the town or city that you live in (we never use street addresses) for our advertising for this book.

Thank you for helping us and, most important, for helping others.

Jack Hartman
Lamplight Publications
P.O. Box 3293
Manchester, NH 03105

Book and Cassette Tape Order Form

To order books and cassette tapes by Jack Hartman, please use this order form:

Book Or Cassette Tape	# of Copies	Total Price
Deep Inner Peace ($4.95 ea.)	_____	$ _____
Trust God For Your Finances ($4.95 ea.)	_____	$ _____
Nuggets Of Faith ($2.50 ea.)	_____	$ _____

Cassette tapes ($4.00 ea. - $3.00 ea.
  (if three or more tapes are ordered).

Check the tapes that you wish to order.

___ 01H   ___ 02H   ___ 03H   ___ 04H   ___ 05H
___ 06H   ___ 07H   ___ 08H   ___ 09H   ___ 10H
___ 11H   ___ 12H   ___ 13H   ___ 14H   ___ 15H
___ 16H   _____ $ _____

Total Price — Books and Tapes		$ _____
Add 10% Postage and Handling		$ _____

Enclosed Check or Money Order
(Please do not send cash) $ _____

Make check payable to: **Lamplight Publications**
Mail order to: **P.O. Box 3293**
Manchester, NH 03105

Please print your name and address **clearly**:

Name _____

Address _____

City _____

State or Province _____

Zip or Postal Code _____

All Canadian and foreign orders must be submitted in U.S. dollars.
Foreign orders are shipped by uninsured surface mail. We ship all orders within 48 hours of receipt of order.
We will give you a full refund on books and cassette tapes if you are dissatisfied in any way.

159